W9-BFV-771

A SHEARWATER BOOK

Life in the Valley of Death

Other Books by Alan Rabinowitz

Jaguar: One Man's Struggle to Establish
the World's First Jaguar Reserve

Chasing the Dragon's Tail:
The Struggle to Save Thailand's Wild Cats

Beyond the Last Village:
A Journey of Discovery in Asia's Forbidden Wilderness

Life in the Valley of Death

THE FIGHT TO SAVE TIGERS IN A LAND OF GUNS, GOLD, AND GREED

ALAN RABINOWITZ

ISLANDPRESS | Shearwater Books

Washington • Covelo • London

A Shearwater Book
Published by Island Press

Copyright © 2008 Alan Rabinowitz

All rights reserved under International and Pan-American Copyright
Conventions. No part of this book may be reproduced in any form or
by any means without permission in writing from the publisher:
Island Press, 1718 Connecticut Ave., NW, Suite 300 Washington, DC 20009.

SHEARWATER BOOKS is a trademark
of The Center for Resource Economics.

Library of Congress Cataloging-in-Publication data.

Rabinowitz, Alan, 1953–
  Life in the valley of death : the fight to save tigers in a land of guns, gold,
and greed / by Alan Rabinowitz.
    p.   cm.
  "A Shearwater Book."
  Includes bibliographical references and index.
  ISBN 978-1-59726-129-6 (hardcover : alk. paper)
  1. Tigers—Conservation—Burma—Hukawng Valley.   2. Rabinowitz, Alan,
1953–   I. Title.
  QL737.C23R33 2008
  333.95'975609591—dc22

                                        2007026190

British Cataloguing-in-Publication data available.

Printed on recycled, acid-free paper ♲

Design by Brighid Willson

Manufactured in the United States of America

10 9 8 7 6 5 4 3 2 1

Keywords: Myanmar, wildlife, Southeast Asia, adventure, cancer, World War II, stuttering.

In memory of my mother, Shirley Rabinowitz,
who passed away in April 2006.

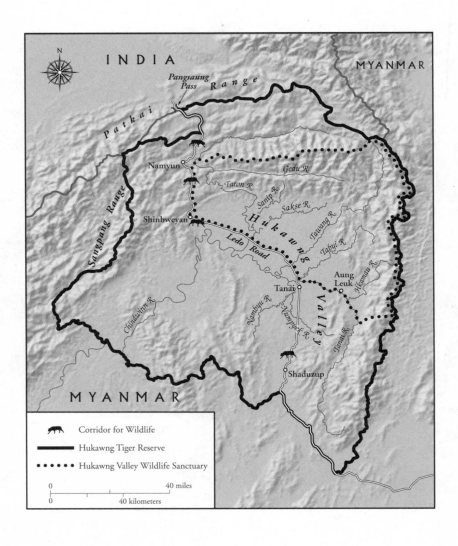

INDIA

MYANMAR

Pangsaung
Pass

Patkai

Range

Namyun

Gedu R.

Taton R.

Samp R.

Sakse R.

Shinbweyan

Sangpang Range

H u k a w n g

Tawang R.

Tabyi R.

Ledo Road

Aung
Leuk

Kamun R.

Tanai

V a l l e y

Chindwinn R.

Nambyu R.

Numpyek R.

Tanai R.

Shaduzup

MYANMAR

Corridor for Wildlife

Hukawng Tiger Reserve

Hukawng Valley Wildlife Sanctuary

| 0 | | | 40 miles |
| 0 | | 40 kilometers | |

Contents

Prologue I

CHAPTER 1
Road to Nowhere 3

CHAPTER 2
Paradise Lost II

CHAPTER 3
The Valley of Death 17

CHAPTER 4
Into the Naga Hills 37

CHAPTER 5
Rolling the Dice 61

CHAPTER 6

Into the Darkness   73

CHAPTER 7

Letting Go   85

CHAPTER 8

Hungry Ghosts   91

CHAPTER 9

Where There Be Tigers   105

CHAPTER 10

Conservation Warfare   117

CHAPTER 11

Jungle Politics   127

CHAPTER 12

Shaping a Miracle   139

CHAPTER 13

A Question of Balance   157

CHAPTER 14

Burning Bright   167

CHAPTER 15
Return to the Naga Hills   177

CHAPTER 16
Spots of Time   187

CHAPTER 17
Reaching Mt. Analogue   197

Selected Bibliography   209

Acknowledgments   213

Index   217

Author's Note

The historic name of the Union of Myanmar until 1989 was Burma. The currently accepted names and spellings for the country and its cities and rivers are used throughout this book except when other authors are quoted or reference is made to a period when the former names were used. The official language of Myanmar is described in this book as Burmese. A distinction, however, should be noted between the Bamar (or Burman) people, who comprise the country's major ethnic group that speaks the Burmese language, and the numerous other ethnic groups in Myanmar.

When the names of Myanmar people are written, *U* (pronounced "oo") is placed before the given name of an adult male, a sign of respectful address and whose literal translation is "uncle. " Similarly, *Daw* means "aunt" and is placed before the name of an adult woman. These customary forms of address are used only the first time that someone's proper name is given.

Prologue

A LION GROWLS in the shadows to my right and I freeze, momentarily frightened. Feeling foolish, I start walking again, shifting a little to the left and trying to act as if nothing untoward has happened.

"Stop being scared so easily," I tell myself, listening to the cacophony of grunts and roars that fill the hall around me. I make a beeline for the spot where I always go when my father brings me here. He hangs back a bit, realizing I have to be by myself. He understands, while not understanding.

Five cages down from the entrance to the Great Cat House at the Bronx Zoo, I stop. The tiger paces, back and forth, back and forth, testicles swinging, mouth opening to a grimace, showing worn yet still impressive canines.

The animal's massive body with long black stripes against an orange background stands in stark contrast to the bare concrete walls that imprison it. Every time I come here, I wonder what these poor animals did to deserve such a fate. Even at the age of eight, I realize that something is terribly wrong. I just don't understand why others around me act as if they can't see it.

"Don't get too close," my father warns, as I lean against the horizontal bar that prevents people from going right up against the cage. I don't respond. How can I? I've spent all my childhood as a severe stutterer, trapped inside my own head, unable to put a complete sentence to a single thought.

I close my eyes, blocking out everything except the feeling of energy, restlessness, and fear coming from the animal in front of me. I am perversely comforted by the thought that this powerful beast is as trapped as I am in this world. Every waking second of every day, we both measure the walls that hold us, looking for a way out. I lean in a little closer, opening my eyes again.

The tiger paces, ignoring me. I don't exist in his world. But he has a large presence in mine.

"There's a place for things like us," I whisper through the bars.

❧ CHAPTER 1 ❧

The Road to Nowhere

Had I been a World War II aficionado, I would have known of the Hukawng Valley long before I first saw it from the air or heard hunters speak of its tigers. I was in Thailand, browsing in a Bangkok bookstore, when I first learned of the connection. A book called *Burma Surgeon Returns* by Gordon Seagrave had just caught my eye.

"You a war buff?" a voice next to me asked.

I turned toward an elderly man with a distinct British accent.

"No, just interested in old books on Burma," I replied.

"Well, you picked a good one there." He nodded at my book. "That was some hell they fought in. I was in Europe myself at the time. Didn't know what those boys were up to over here. We had our own problems. But that road that Stilwell put through the jungle —my word! Most people have no idea what he and those boys went through."

I nodded empathetically, though I had no idea what he was talking about. Then I bought the book.

Tales of intrigue, terror, and death from the jungles of the Hukawng Valley, an area of thousands of square miles in northwest Myanmar bordering the Indian state of Assam, in fact date back centuries. The valley's original name, *ju-kaung*, came from the

Jinghpaw dialect of the Kachin people, who dominated the region. The word means "cremation mounds," referring to the deaths that occurred when the Kachin systematically pushed out or enslaved other ethnic groups in the area—the Shan, the Chin, and the Palaung.

The Patkai Mountain Range, bordering the valley to the west, was the site of continual battles between kingdoms in Burma and Assam during the fourteenth century. A peace treaty in AD 1401 made these mountains the boundary separating the warring kingdoms, and four centuries later, in 1837, the British, who by then controlled much of the region, fixed the same range as the official border between India and Burma. Continual incursions by the Burmese into Assam finally led the British to annex all of Burma in 1885.

Some of the earliest official reports of the Hukawng Valley to reach the West came from British expeditions in the 1830s and '40s sent to survey the region or investigate disputes of Kachin chieftains in what Great Britain termed the "unadministered territory between Upper Chindwin and the Naga Hills." Early mentions are made of salt, gold, and an abundance of wild game in the valley, particularly tigers and elephants. One of the most valued commodities at the time was amber, which the Kachin mined in the Hukawng and sold to the Chinese.

Although the Hukawng Valley had been a battleground for centuries, it took World War II to make it infamous in the annals of history. By the summer of 1942, as the Japanese swept northward through much of Burma, a small tribal footpath through the Hukawng Valley had become a major escape route for many locals and Allied soldiers. Fleeing through the dense jungles toward the border with India, few among them were prepared for the scorching heat, torrential downpours, cold nights, omnipresent leeches, biting flies, and then the rugged, 10,000-foot mountains separating Burma from India. Thousands of corpses of women, children, and soldiers littered the trail.

By late May 1942, the Japanese had reached the beginning of

the 700-mile Burma Road, which ran from the railhead at Lashio in Burma to the city of Kunming in China, cutting the only overland supply route to General Chiang Kai-shek's Allied base. As the Japanese continued farther northward, moving forces into the lower Hukawng Valley, the battered escape route that had taken so many lives became known as the most hazardous refugee trail in the world. Some of the crossings of the shallow streams in the valley had human skulls as stepping-stones. Even the fearsome Naga people, who had lived in the Hukawng Valley for centuries, decided to move deeper into the jungle, believing the trail cursed.

With the only land route for supplies from the West cut off, Chiang Kai-shek's forces became increasingly isolated in China. While the main military effort of the Allies was directed toward defeating Nazi Germany, China still had to be supplied if Japan was to be stopped from sweeping over Asia. It was Chiang Kai-shek himself who first suggested the building of a new land route to China that would start in the Indian town of Ledo, descend the mountains bordering Assam, and, with military support, snake through the dense lowland jungle of the Hukawng Valley, ultimately linking to the Burma Road above Lashio.

Winston Churchill dismissed the idea of the Ledo Road as foolish, "an immense, laborious task, unlikely to be finished before the need for it had passed," and likened the retaking of northern Burma from the Japanese to munching on a porcupine, quill by quill. The commander of America's engineers based in Ledo at the time claimed that building such a road would be "the toughest engineering job on the planet." But a fiery American general, "Vinegar Joe" Stilwell, was undeterred. Self-described as unreasonable, impatient, sullen, mad, profane, and vulgar, Stilwell was a man known to take on what others considered impossible. He had been rushed to the Far East by President Franklin D. Roosevelt out of concern that China might drop out of the war against Japan. His job was to command the small number of U.S. troops in China and

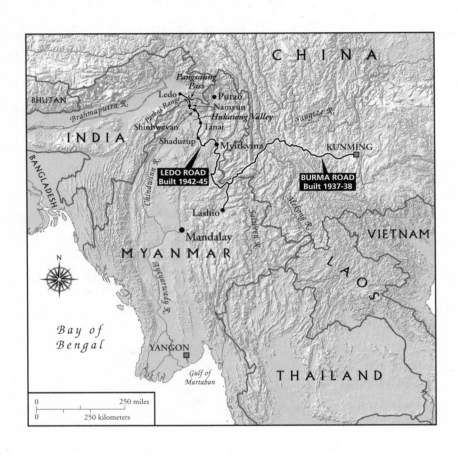

to oversee the shipment of thousands of tons of American war materials to Chiang Kai-shek. By the time Stilwell arrived for his new assignment, the Japanese army had already conquered much of Burma, so Vinegar Joe decided he must retake the Burma Road and push forward with plans for the Ledo Road.

For more than two years, as many as 17,000 engineers overseeing 50,000 to 60,000 laborers worked twenty-four hours a day, seven days a week, to build the 478-mile, 30-foot-wide all-weather track from India to the old Burma Road and its route to China. Seven hundred bridges and up to 13 culverts per mile were constructed over 10 major rivers and 155 streams while negotiating steep defiles, gorges, and raging rapids. Six oil and gas pipelines were also laid down along the road. As American engineers ducked sniper fire, a contingent of Chinese soldiers stayed out in front of them to retake the route out of the valley. Through it all, Stilwell was adamant in his resolve to complete what he now called "the path to Hell."

Touted as the greatest engineering feat of the war, what Chiang Kai-shek started calling the Stilwell Road cost $150 million (in the currency of the time), with an estimated human toll of "a man a mile." Yet Churchill's words had been prophetic. The Ledo Road was deemed obsolete before it was finished and became passable only seven months before the war ended. It was used twice by Allied convoys.

But even as work began on the road, Chiang Kai-shek's forces still needed to be supplied. In 1942, Roosevelt authorized the creation of the Air Transport Command. Using C-46 cargo planes, pilots flew 12,000 tons of supplies a month over the Himalayan "Hump," an air route crossing the 10,000- to 20,000-foot mountains of India, Burma, and China, including the Naga Hills that enclosed the northern Hukawng Valley. This was the first time in military history that an entire nation's armed forces were supplied by air.

Flying the Hump, like building the Ledo Road, came at a high

cost. Monsoon winds of up to 250 miles per hour, along with blind-
ing rains, snow, and ice, caused pilots to call the runs over these
mountains Operation Vomit. With no navigational aids and frequent
anti-aircraft fire, an average of eight planes a month crashed into the
jungles of the Hukawng. Some pilots said they could find their way
from India to China just by the trail of downed aircraft on the
ground. By the time the war ended, nearly 600 planes had gone
down, with more than 1,000 Hump fliers listed as dead or missing in
action on what was called World War II's most treacherous air route.

I HAVE BEEN CONTINUALLY AMAZED by what I've learned of the
Hukawng Valley since I started to dig for information and explore
the area on the ground in the years since that encounter in a
Bangkok bookstore. It still seems incongruous that this remote
no-man's-land in the foothills of the Himalayas, perhaps one of
Southeast Asia's last strongholds for tigers and other big mammals,
was once talked about by luminaries such as Franklin Roosevelt,
Winston Churchill, Chiang Kai-shek, Mao Tse-tung, and Lord
Mountbatten. Or that its dense jungles and snaking waterways were
the sites of the legendary and heroic military feats of Wingate's
Chindits and Merrill's Marauders. British refugees fleeing for their
lives from the Japanese advance called the Hukawng the Valley of
Death; American soldiers building the Ledo Road called it Green
Hell; pilots flying the Hump prayed that the dense jungles below
would not be their final resting place.

Yet through it all life in this valley persevered. Even in the
midst of so much death, one American soldier recalled the jungles
of the Hukawng as "wild and beautiful with a savage heart," a place
where one was continually "in the midst of tigers, black leopards,
cobras, pythons, and monkeys." An Australian child who lost his
entire family as they fled the Japanese along the early refugee trail
through the valley, despite all, still recalled as an adult the clean,

cold Himalayan rivers, the beautiful blue-green mountains, and animals in abundance. Everything about this Valley of Death seemed out of some macabre fiction. Yet very soon this remote valley was to consume me and become the focus of my life for nearly a decade.

❧ CHAPTER 2 ❧

Paradise Lost

THE FOKKER F-28 lurched left as I tried to quell thoughts of the tourist warnings against flying Myanmar Air, the domestic carrier of this country. I pressed my face against the window, but the cloudless blue sky and the steady hum of the plane's propellers belied any fears of trouble. Then when I looked down, all concerns were momentarily forgotten. Below me lay an endless sea of forest green stretching west and disappearing into distant mists. Rising from the mists were gleaming, seemingly chimerical snow-capped peaks. On this day in March 1996, I could scarcely imagine that ten years later I'd be in those very forests, fighting to save the home of one of the most majestic species ever to walk the face of the earth.

"Those are the Patkai and Sangpawng Mountains in the distance," U Saw Tun Khaing said, following my gaze. "India's on the other side. All that jungle is the Hukawng Valley. Not much there now but malaria and corpses." The fit fifty-three-year-old I'd recently hired to run the Myanmar program for the Wildlife Conservation Society (WCS) turned his worn face back to the magazine he was reading.

I leaned back and closed my eyes for a moment. I'd known Saw

Tun Khaing only a short time, but his soft voice and gentle demeanor comforted me. A former deputy director of the Myanmar Forest Department with a master's degree in forestry from the University of Aberdeen, Scotland, and a devout Buddhist, he had proven his worth to me from the outset, using his myriad of contacts with the government to get things done. By now I realized how much I depended on him.

It hadn't been that way during my first two years in Myanmar, though. With no one to turn to for personal or professional advice, I did whatever I thought it took just to stay in the country and gain the trust of its leaders. At the government's request, I held wildlife research training courses for Forest Department staff, I searched for the last Sumatran rhinos near the Indian border, and I surveyed the largest uninhabited island in the Mergui Archipelago, setting it up as the country's first marine national park. Keeping armed soldiers from trampling animal tracks, interviewing Naga villagers, and squeezing into the cramped living quarters on the boats of the Moken, one of the world's last nomadic, sea-based cultures, I began to learn how rich the natural and social history of this land was.

Myanmar's history and people are an integral part of the complex mosaic that makes up modern-day Southeast Asia. The region was first populated by migrants moving southward from Tibet, and one of the earliest references to its people appears in Ptolemy's *Geographia Syntaxis* (AD 125), which claimed that lower Burma was inhabited by "cannibals and white-skinned, flat nosed, hairy dwarfs." But by the eleventh century these so-called cannibals and dwarfs had created one of the world's most powerful kingdoms, ruling much of the region from a vast capital city complex called Bagan, situated along the Ayeyarwady River in the dry central plains ninety miles southwest of the city of Mandalay, itself the last capital of the last independent Burmese kingdom before annexation by the British. With more than 13,000 Buddhist temples and monuments, the glory of Bagan was to last almost 300 years and span several ancient kingdoms, until it was finally sacked by the Mongol armies of Kubla Khan in 1287. When Marco Polo visited the site twelve years after it was ravaged, he wrote that the temples of Bagan still "form one of the finest sights in the world."

While Bagan would never regain its former glory, it contributed to the building of a nation that by the first decades of the twentieth century, while still under British rule, was called the Golden Land and had one of the richest economies in all of Asia. In the early 1900s, Myanmar was also a major destination for the sport hunting of large mammals, promoted by publications such as *Big Game Shooting in Upper Burma* by Major C. P. Evans and *A Gamebook for Burma and Adjoining Territories* by E. H. Peacock, which described the dense forests and abundant wildlife of the country in flamboyant terms.

But political instability, insurgency, and heavy-handed military regimes following World War II sent the nation, known to many as Burma until its name was changed to Myanmar in 1989, into a decline that put it on the list of the ten poorest countries in the world and kept people from traveling safely through the countryside for decades. The nation as a whole remained remarkably rich in wildlife, however. At last count, the 1,200-mile-long piece of land that is Myanmar, sandwiched between India and Thailand, was believed to have at least 7,000 species of plants, 300 species of mammals, 360 species of reptiles, and 1,000 species of birds. But the status of these plant and animal populations after the tumultuous decades following independence from Britain in 1948 was anyone's guess. That's why I'd come here.

I put my face to the window again. We were hundreds of miles beyond the ancient capital of Bagan now, and almost 800 miles from the capital of Yangon, where I had started my trip. My destination was Putao, the northernmost city accessible by air and the country's gateway to the Himalayas. Having focused so long on gaining permission to explore the roadless region of subalpine habitats and snowy Himalayan mountaintops between Putao and Tibet, I'd forgotten how vast and unexplored were the dense jungles we were now passing over, scene of so much history. I pulled a topographic map of Myanmar from my pack to help orient myself. The Ledo Road, I noticed, wasn't even depicted now.

Below me lay the vast 35,000 square miles of Kachin State, the northernmost region in Myanmar, an appendage-like piece of land almost the size of Portugal jutting between China and India. With only about thirty people per square mile and spanning elevations of 500 to 20,000 feet, this extraordinary region contains some of the most extensive forests and intact wildlife habitats in the Indo-Pacific, much of it in the Hukawng Valley. This was—or at least had been—tiger country we were flying over, that I knew. But with permits for another region finally in hand, I was heading into the high snowcapped mountains in the distance that likely contained, if not tigers, other fascinating and threatened species that few people have ever seen: the colorful red pandas, the oxlike takin, the primitive tusked musk deer, and the goat-like goral. Had a tiger ever killed a 1,000-pound takin, I wondered? I pulled my notepad from my shirt pocket and started to jot down some thoughts when, suddenly, my stomach bottomed out. The captain announced that we'd started our descent.

THOUGHTS OF THAT FIRST SIGHTING of the Hukawng Valley were put aside for the next two years as I fulfilled my dream of exploring the remote northern mountains bordering Tibet and India. I recounted those explorations—including the discovery of little-known Himalayan species and my encounters with people from some of Myanmar's least-known ethnic groups, including the Rawang, the Htalu, and the nearly extinct Taron, the world's only pygmies of Mongoloid descent—in a book, *Beyond the Last Village: A Journey of Discovery in Asia's Forbidden Wilderness*. As a result of those efforts, Burmese colleagues and I were able to persuade the government to establish Mount Hkakabo Razi National Park, a 1,500-square-mile protected area at the northern tip of the country.

Throughout those early surveys, the Hukawng Valley kept popping up on the lips of hunters and shopkeepers in Putao or other village markets whenever I inquired about large mammals such as tigers, elephants, gaur, or clouded leopards. When I asked why I saw no sign of the elephants and tigers that should live in Putao's surrounding forested valleys and foothills, the answer was always the same: only the village elders had memories of such animals. Those that were once there had all been killed.

From the time I first set foot in Myanmar, I knew it was the tigers I would ultimately want to seek. With a record weight of nearly 850 pounds, this behemoth of the cat world once ranged across much of Asia: from eastern Turkey, into the forests south of the Tibetan Plateau, to Manchuria and the Russian Far East, up to elevations of 12,000 feet. But their numbers were in steep decline. At the beginning of the twentieth century, perhaps as many as 100,000 tigers still roamed the earth. By the end of the century, it was rare to meet anyone anywhere who had encountered a tiger in the wild.

"They still live in the Hukawng," one old Lisu headman in a village north of Putao told me through an interpreter. Showing me an old tiger-skin pouch, he spoke of the Hukawng Valley almost reverently. "I hunted there once, many years ago." Then he pointed toward distant mountains to the southwest with a slight shake of the head, as if I were asking about the unknowable. "It's a hard place."

I looked around me. This man was surviving on the edge of civilization, I thought, scraping a living from the shallow soil and rock of the area, trading wildlife skins for tea, salt, and a few other essentials that his people need to survive. Yet the way he and his countrymen spoke of the Hukawng Valley and the distant mountains along the India border, it was as if I were asking after Mount Analogue, the fictitious mountain in French poet René Daumal's unfinished novel that was hidden from human sight, with a peak so high it remained inaccessible. Daumal's mountain could be reached only by those "for whom the impossible no longer existed." I liked the idea. But I didn't realize at the time that the idyllic Garden of Eden I pictured developing again in the Hukawng Valley after the war would turn out to be more akin to Dante's Inferno. The real story behind this valley, I was learning, was darker and far more interesting than any fiction.

⚑ CHAPTER 3 ⚐

The Valley of Death

"**Y**OU HAVE TO SIGN a release form," the Forest Department official says to me. It is March 1999, and the Ministry of Defense has finally granted me permission to visit the Hukawng Valley itself. As with my earlier expeditions in Myanmar, I had proposed to the government that I would survey this little-known area to assess its value as a possible protected area, paying particular attention to the presence of tigers, elephants, and rhinos.

"The government cannot be responsible for what happens to you," he continues.

"When have they ever felt responsible for me?" I turn and say in English to Saw Tun Khaing, who is standing beside me. He shrugs and smiles, as if to say, "Why are you even bothering to ask such questions?"

Since I have spent the past five years traveling to some of Myanmar's most remote areas, I wonder where this sudden insistence on a release form is coming from. Perhaps it was the helicopter mishap that nearly cost our lives in the Hkakabo Razi region during our 1997 expedition. I'd heard that the minister of defense was quite irritated about the circumstances of our "hard landing" and was never given the full story by his subordinates. Still, this sudden

17

concern for my welfare seems a bit unnerving. Maybe the Hukawng has everyone spooked.

The Forest Department officials apologize to me repeatedly, explaining that they are just following orders. I sympathize with these dedicated men, whose department was once the envy of Asia. Sadly, its fate has been tied to the country's shifting political fortunes. Now, as my footsteps echo in the hallways of the spacious, mostly empty and unkept buildings, I remind myself that while Forestry is still one of the most profitable ministries in the government, few of those funds reach these offices.

Most of the Forest Department staff I know are paid such low wages (the director-general was making less than $25 per month when I first arrived in the country) that they are barely able to eke out a living, much less do the jobs they were trained for. Feeling powerless, and with no expectation of change anytime soon, many of the younger staff in the department have developed businesses on the side or taken second jobs to pay the bills. Few have ever been far from their offices in the capital city of Yangon, and some have never even been to the forest.

Two months after receiving permission to explore the Hukawng Valley, I fly to the closest city, Myitkyina, with a team of Forest Department and WCS field staff. By now, both Saw Tun Khaing and the man he has hired to co-direct our Myanmar program, U Than Myint, have the organization of our backcountry trips down to a science. This is no small accomplishment, given the restrictions on foreigners in this nation. But with each passing year, and with each successful trip with the Forest Department, I gain more of the government's trust.

This is already evident in the evolution of the regime's military intelligence (MI) operation that continually tracks and reports on my movements outside Yangon. On this trip I am down to only one MI officer, and he is quiet and unobtrusive, happy to stay in the background. It's a far cry from earlier trips. When I surveyed for Sumatran rhinos up the Chindwinn River in Tamanthi

Wildlife Sanctuary, an entire platoon of soldiers accompanied me. They surrounded my sleeping area at night and followed me into the woods when I had to relieve myself. Only the sight of my bare buttocks kept them at bay.

The flight to Myitkyina via Mandalay is delayed several hours due to a malfunctioning engine. I pop a five-milligram Valium tablet into my mouth to stop the butterflies in my gut from worsening and my palms from sweating. More than two decades in the field and too many close calls have taken their toll on my psyche. A small-plane crash, a subdural hematoma, and a worker killed by a poisonous fer-de-lance bite in the jungles of Belize while studying jaguars; a bamboo punji stick trap stabbed through my left foot and one of our forest staff killed in a shootout with poachers while tracking leopards in Thailand; a machete slash in Borneo by a drunken local who thought I had insulted him; a helicopter malfunction and near collision with a mountain in the Himalayan foothills of northern Myanmar. I have lost track of the parasites and illnesses. My fears magnify, not lessen, with the years. How often can one spin the wheel of fate, I wonder?

The seats in the plane have a musty, unclean smell. As the flight attendant walks the aisle offering airsickness bags, I watch a large spider crawl along the armrest of the person sitting in front of me. As the plane lifts off, rain and turbulence buffet us. Some of passengers grip the armrests tightly, as if they too think each trip on Myanmar Air is a crapshoot. The spider is squashed. I can hear the sound of someone using one of the vomit bags.

We land in Myitkyina by late afternoon. Half a century earlier this city, now Myanmar's third largest and located 1,000 miles north of Yangon, was a major battleground as Allied forces pushed the Japanese out of the Hukawng Valley and fought to take back control of northern Burma and the Burma Road. Now, with nearly 150,000 people, horse-drawn carriages and bicycles still share the streets with pickup trucks, most of them made in China. But the seeming charm of this capital of Kachin State hides tension that simmers just below the surface.

Military bases and armed soldiers from the central government are everywhere evident because Myitkyina is headquarters to the Kachin Independent Army (KIA), the largest of the insurgent groups fighting for independence. Formed in 1961 with only a few World War II rifles and the dream of establishing a free Kachin republic, this fledgling army, which bartered jade and opium for goods and weapons from neighboring countries, soon became a force to be reckoned with. During the 1970s the KIA's influence grew so substantially that a political and administrative wing was formed, the Kachin Independent Organization (KIO). Tensions boiled over in 1986 when a Myanmar regional military commander was gunned down in the streets of Myitkyina.

During the late 1980s and early 1990s the military government signed cease-fire agreements with twenty-two armed ethnic opposition groups throughout the country. A cease-fire agreement with the KIO/KIA was signed only in 1994, and the idea of peaceful coexistence with the current regime was still being tested. In the meantime, the KIA was able to keep its weapons and maintain its recruitment camps. One of the largest of the KIA's armed jungle bases, I'd learned only recently, was located inside the Hukawng Valley.

Two Toyota trucks are waiting to take us on the ten-hour, 122-mile drive west from Myitkyina and then north along the Ledo Road to the town of Tanai, the largest settlement deep inside the Hukawng Valley. While the road is not as the Americans left it fifty-four years earlier, it is surprisingly intact. But after hitting one too many potholes, one of our trucks loses a steering rod. We squeeze everyone into the remaining vehicle and leave the driver with the damaged truck to catch up when he can.

Village settlements dot the roadside, mostly simple wooden shacks built on high ground or raised up on posts, sometimes with a schoolhouse, always with a church at the center of the enclave. Throughout Kachin State, Christian missionaries long since replaced animism with monotheism as the prevailing belief. Now some people feel they have a God-given mandate to use and dominate the earth in whatever way suits them. North of Putao, local preachers often encourage hunting, collecting their tithe in animal skins that they then sell to traders. I am mollified a bit by the occasional sight of large posts tied together in the shape of an X, often with a buffalo or cow head attached. Such structures, remnants of the past, appease the troublesome local animistic spirits called *nats*.

There is little forest along this section of the Ledo Road. The land is mostly flat, with dense greenery visible in the distance. Around the villages are rice paddies or second-growth vegetation from old slash-and-burn fields. Also termed swidden agriculture, this destructive practice of cutting down and burning the forest for planting is common throughout much of tropical Southeast Asia. The burnt ash provides some fertilizer, and the plot is relatively free of weeds the first year. But after several seasons on relatively shallow soils, the weeds proliferate and the fertility of the site declines until the farmer is forced to cut and burn new areas of forest, waiting perhaps seven years until returning to an old site. But on each return, the soil is often more degraded and less fertile. In areas on sloping hills, topsoil is washed away during rainy season and the site degrades much faster.

Beyond the fields, however, lie some of the most threatened habitats in all of tropical Asia, natural grasslands and wetlands. Rich in wildlife, these are usually the first areas to be developed or taken over for agriculture. Beyond the grasslands, a backdrop of mountains shelters the valley on all sides, lending some plausibility to the theory of a British explorer who thought that the Hukawng Valley originated as the ancient bed of an alpine lake. There are few other vehicles on the road; most people travel on foot, bicycle, or sometimes elephant. It is a bucolic setting mostly undisturbed by modern development, with few apparent scars despite its violent past.

The town of Tanai itself surprises me. It is a bustling frontier settlement with several thousand people and none of the quiet charm that I associate with other remote towns in Myanmar. Instead, it has the energy of a New York City street corner. People seem hurried and self-absorbed. Young girls with stylishly cut hair walk barefoot in the muddy roads, while men sit at outdoor food stalls sharing bottles of expensive brandy in the early afternoon.

Drunken altercations are a nightly occurrence, and we are warned not to wander the streets after dark. Many of the people, I learn, are transients. During the five- to six-month dry season, which starts around October and has just ended, large numbers of people enter the valley to strip the forests of its bamboo, rattan, aloe wood, amber, and gold, then return home again when the torrential rains begin.

Having no prearranged accommodation, we are given permission by town authorities to sleep in the schoolhouse. The next morning we make the obligatory rounds: visits to the local army commander, the police chief, and the township chairman. At each stop we present our paperwork and explain the purpose of our trip. Everyone already knows of our coming and why we are here. We just have to go through the motions. The military assigns a new man to accompany us and report on my activities.

At the edge of town, the Tanai River, a major tributary of the Chindwinn, marks the end of the drivable road, separating the accessible world from the inaccessible. With nearly a 1,000-foot span between banks, only the twisted metal supports jutting up from the water provide evidence of the bridge that once stood there, built by the Americans during World War II. I'm told that almost all of the bridges over the hundreds of rivers and small streams from this point onward have been washed away, are in disrepair, or were destroyed by the KIA when they were fighting against the government.

A boat carries us across and we now start hoofing it along the Ledo Road, which here is overgrown and potholed and almost disappears in places. It appears virtually impassable except on foot, and I wonder how much it resembles the old refugee path of World

War II. Over the next two weeks we walk, boat, and ride elephants nearly 150 miles through the Hukawng Valley, sometimes passing discarded, rusting sections of the pipelines that once carried fuel along the road from India to China, and other times passing the remains of an old jeep or truck long discarded on the side of the road.

With the rainy season only just now starting, the weather alternates between battering rains and scorching sun. I curse the sun when it burns into my skull and bakes my brain; then I rage against the relentless rain when it soaks me to the skin, brings out the leeches, and makes my steps heavy. Within days my armpits and groin are irritated from the constant rubbing of wet cloth against skin. While the rainy season is generally not an ideal time to travel in the forest, I prefer the rain to the sun. I decide that I am even glad to see the leeches, despite the bloody havoc they wreak on my legs after I dislodge them with a stick or cigarette lighter. It means that lots of warm-blooded animals, other than humans, are around too.

The local people here believe that the Hukawng Valley, surrounded as it is by high mountains, creates its own weather. With nearly 150 inches of rain falling between May and October, this valley has one of the highest annual rainfalls in the world. The result is nearly 5,600 square miles of fertile alluvial plain covered mostly with dense evergreen forests. Seasonal inundation of the lowlands during much of the year makes agriculture all but impossible in many areas of the valley, turning the jungle into a swamp. This wall of dense greenery that now surrounds me is what had first caught my eye from the plane on my way to Putao five years earlier.

Mostly Kachin live in the valley, with small groups of Lisu and Shan in the lowlands, and the feared Naga up in the mountains. Disease and heavy rainfall have brought many of the human settlements close to the Ledo Road, where the land is more elevated and there is greater ease of access. Rice is the staple crop, but I also pass by patches of tapioca, maize, yams, corn, and pumpkins. Sometimes

I see a small, colorful private garden with bananas, grapefruits, and limes, fenced in with metal sheets fashioned from salvaged oil drums, another reminder of the war.

Settlements of any size are scarce after leaving Tanai. Despite some semblance of the road, access is still difficult, and the incidence of malaria and tuberculosis is high. Few people along here ever seek medical treatment, even in Tanai. Pharmaceuticals of any kind require money and are hard to come by, so traditional treatments are the norm. Opium is frequently the medicine of choice.

The men who fought in the Hukawng during World War II learned quickly to both respect and fear the Kachin. Angered by the Japanese treatment of the region's people, the Kachin readily fought alongside Allied forces. Using traditional crossbows as well as guns, the Kachin were adept jungle fighters who liked to shoot Japanese only to wound them so that they could then charge forward and finish the soldiers off with a knife, just as they hunted wild pigs in the forest. Along remote mountain trails, the Kachin would place carefully hidden sharpened bamboo stakes. When a Japanese patrol neared, they would fire weapons and make noise, forcing the soldiers to dive for cover and spear themselves with the stakes. What terrified the Japanese most, however, was the Kachin habit of keeping track of their kills by slicing off and keeping the ears of their victims. But for an Allied soldier who was lost or injured in the jungle, the sight of a Kachin could mean life itself: more than 700 pilots and crew members who went down while flying the Hump during the war were rescued by the Kachin.

Whether it is because the purpose of our team seems suspect, or because my ethnicity is associated with a violent past, few local people anywhere in this valley welcome our presence. This is in stark contrast to my previous trips in Myanmar, where children ran out to greet us and villagers welcomed us into their homes. Here we are often met with silence and closed doors. Although the people of the region are clearly in desperate need of money and goods, most are reluctant to rent us their domesticated elephants and even

fewer wish to hire on as porters. Sometimes when a village headman assigns porters for us, they run off in the middle of the night
and then the headman himself disappears.

Though my first impression from the air of a huge valley
devoid of people has been dispelled, my hope of finding a large
expanse of intact forest and natural habitats filled with wildlife is
more than satisfied. Old washed-out tire tracks along the Ledo
Road are replaced with tracks of tigers, clouded leopards, and wild
dogs as we head farther into the backcountry. In the early morn-
ings I am serenaded by the melodic calls of Hoolock's gibbons,
while at night I hear the occasional wild elephant trumpeting in
the distance. Flocks of hornbills or troops of macaques often burst
from the canopy when we pass. Along the rivers, bear, wild pig, and
deer sign are common; when on foot or in boats, we are treated to
periodic sightings of the endangered woolly-necked stork and
white-bellied heron, or the threatened white-winged wood duck,
green peafowl, and spot-billed pelican. Only rhino are missing
from the scene, with the last reliable sighting in the valley dating
back to 1935. Tasked with helping the Myanmar Forest Department find wild areas worthy of protection, Hukawng Valley now
sits at the top of my list.

Eventually we acquire six elephants for our expedition. But my
fantasy of riding through the jungle like some maharaja is quickly
dispelled when I realize how much easier and less bone-jarring it is
to walk. Also, since several of our elephant handlers, called mahouts,
are addicted to opium, an early morning start is not part of their
repertoire. So we use the elephants in place of porters to carry our
supplies. This allows the mahouts to move at their own pace and
catch up to us long after we arrive at our next camp.

I never tire of having the elephants with us. Although I prefer
to see them in the wild, Asian elephants have been captured, tamed,

and worked by humans for more than 4,000 years. While many of the common myths about elephants—they never forget, they fear mice, they drink through their tusks, they have a graveyard where they go to die—have no basis in fact, something about the world's largest land mammal fires the imagination.

The pleasure I get from being close to them, smelling their musky scent and touching their thick, rough skin, seems primordial. Our group includes only one male elephant, with two-foot-long tusks. Unlike the elephants of Africa, female Asian elephants have no tusks. In any case, it is rare to find even male tuskers in the jungle these days. Life expectancy is shortened considerably when "white gold" protrudes from your head.

Sometimes in the evening I visit with one young female elephant whom I've grown attached to. When I approach, I stop about two feet away and then turn my back, as if ignoring her. Very soon I feel the breeze from her flapping ears. Then I feel the tip of her trunk moving up and down my body, exploring for the treat she knows I've brought her. If I make it too difficult, she grabs at bits of my clothes using the tip of her trunk like a hand. I smile whenever I think of this hulking several-ton beast—with a brain four times the size of a human's, and a proboscis containing 40,000 muscles and tendons that can rip a tree from the ground—touching, prodding, and grabbing at me with a touch as gentle as a woman's caress.

Three young Naga teens, ages fifteen, eighteen, and nineteen, join our group as porters, wanting, they say, to make some money while returning to their villages in the mountains. The youngest runs off after a few days, taking with him some extra rice. But we also acquire two young Kachin girls, one with a noticeable goiter on her neck, as cooks. Both porters and cooks are paid 400 kyat per day (approximately US$1 at the time), half the rate we are paying for the elephants. I have no say in these matters, and if I try to interfere, I am admonished by Saw Tun Khaing. Short-term generosity does little to help, he is quick to remind me. It throws customary relationships off balance.

I rarely see Saw Tun Khaing annoyed. He reminds me more of a Buddhist monk than of a former government official. But the Hukawng seems to continually put him in a sour mood.

"These are not people of Myanmar," he says one morning after two more porters run off and the village headman is nowhere to be found. "Something is wrong with these people. Something is wrong with this place."

I agree. There is something "off" about the Hukawng, with its history as a battleground, a bloody testament to human cruelty. It's as if the people here have not gone through the normal social evolution that characterizes most areas of long-term human settlement. But it doesn't bother me as much as it does Saw Tun Khaing. I'd found what I was most seeking. I'd found tigers.

I stop in the village of Makaw, where both tiger and leopard have been reported recently. I ask after the headman, who then invites us in for tea.

"There were lots more villages deep inside the valley twenty to thirty years ago. Lots more tigers, too," he comments. "Now the villages are mostly gone and the tigers are a lot fewer. For the people, it's easier to be by the road."

The headman sits on an Asiatic black bear skin. Behind him, racks of sambar deer antlers and skins of a three-striped palm civet and a binturong are tacked to the wall.

Although I've seen few people since we crossed the Tanai River, hunting is still a way of life everywhere in the valley, and certain animals are targeted more than others. When rice harvests are insufficient, people depend on what they can get from the forest, or they pan in the rivers for the small amounts of gold known for generations to be found in this valley. Local hunters travel up to six to seven miles from their village to go after sambar deer, barking deer, wild pig, and gaur.

Some hunters still use traditional crossbows with arrows made from split bamboo, thirteen to fifteen inches long and coated with poison obtained from a tuber of a local plant of the genus *Aconitum*, commonly known as monk's hood or wolf's bane and found only in temperate zones at elevations between 8,000 and 10,000 feet. Others hunt with homemade black powder and flintlock guns. The danger from explosions with these guns is evidenced by the facial scars or missing fingers of some hunters. Snares made from metal cable or vines are also used, usually along the perimeter of paddy fields to catch smaller animals, such as porcupine, civets, and barking deer, all considered pests. The meat from most of these species is eaten or bartered, and deer skins are sold in Tanai or Myitkyina to be made into leather coats.

I find no evidence of significant cross-border wildlife trade with India, especially compared to what I'd seen farther north along the China border. Still, many animals are being killed. Hunters acknowledge that most species are scarcer than they were five years ago. Interestingly, while most adult men hunt, they all blame the decreased numbers of big animals, especially tigers and elephants, on one group of people in particular—the Lisu. Day after day we visit villages along the Ledo Road, occupied mostly by Kachin. People I speak with repeatedly point the finger at organized groups of Lisu hunters that, they say, have been coming into the Hukawng Valley from Putao after tigers for decades. They also hunt gaur and elephants, I'm told. Around 1980 the market demand shifted more toward turtles and otters, though tigers were still sought after. Almost everything that moved became fair game for the hunters.

I know the Lisu well from our previous expeditions into the Tamanthi Wildlife Sanctuary, situated several miles south of the Hukawng Valley along the Chindwinn River. In Tamanthi, the soldiers I traveled with captured a Lisu hunter, for example, one of a small group who came there every year after tigers. While waiting for his tiger traps to work, we encountered him setting smaller snares in the river for otter. His basket was filled with otter skins and penises, all of which he told us were bound for China. He confirmed what our survey at the time had already shown us: there were almost no more tigers left in that 232-square-mile reserve.

But in the vast landscape of the Hukawng Valley, there are still many good indicators of an intact forest and relatively healthy wildlife populations despite current hunting pressures. The fact that I am finding tiger and other wildlife tracks along the road and along stream banks away from villages is a good sign. But I have also tempered my initial enthusiasm. Now I realize that despite the animals I see or hear evidence of around me, I should be finding much more sign of large mammals than I actually am. And the fact that most local villagers no longer fear the large, potentially dangerous animals also indicates that not many are around anymore. Tigers and other species were more abundant here in the past than they are now, many reports are indicating.

The most glaring example of this decline is the valley's wild elephant population. Upon arriving in Tanai, I had learned of an elephant capture committee formed in 1962 that maintained a captive herd of about a hundred elephants. While both the committee's existence and their imprisonment of elephants are illegal without special government permits, the practice has the tacit approval of military and township officials, who appropriate the animals when needed for work crews.

That first evening in the town, I had met with some members of the capture committee. They were not at all what I'd expected. Appearing bedraggled and downtrodden, they were worried, even fearful, of talking with me. Once they understood that it was not my intent to cause trouble for them, however, they readily answered my questions.

"Twenty years ago there were many wild elephants here," the leader said. "The groups were big, and we could catch what we wanted. Usually we took about ten elephants a year. But now, only small groups are left. We get only three or four a year because the numbers are so low. This year was good: we got five elephants."

"Why are the numbers lower now?" I ask, wondering how honest they'll be with me.

"While we only capture elephants, others kill them. The Lisu are very good at killing elephants. They use special poison arrows and poison arrow traps. They even sometimes kill our captive elephants," he said.

In some of the villages I visit along the Ledo Road, Lisu hunters show me what the capture committee had described: special elephant darts made from a wooden shaft shaped to fit the barrel of their rifles. On the end of the darts are metal arrow tips coated in aconite, the same poison used for their crossbow arrows.

"Why do you kill elephants?" I ask repeatedly.

"We can sell the tusks, and sometimes the skin and the genitals," is the most common answer. "It goes to China."

One old elephant hunter regales me with stories of capturing more than a hundred wild elephants during his lifetime. Some he caught by approaching them on a domestic elephant and lassoing them. Usually, however, he and his fellows would just herd them into a "kedah"—a large enclosure built in the forest for the purpose. It sounded like the capture of wild mustangs in the American West.

"We sold the elephants to the timber companies for 1,200 kyats per foot, measured from the toe to the shoulder," he says. "Good money, but too much trouble now. I pan for gold instead."

"How many elephants do you think are still alive in the Hukawng now?" I ask him.

He talks with some others who have gathered nearby.

"Maybe twenty-five years ago there were 1,000 elephants," he says. Some of us remember groups of 200. Now, from Tanai to Shinbweyan (another town fifty miles to the north), maybe eighty to ninety elephants left. Sometimes we will see groups of ten elephants, but usually only four or eight. Maybe there are still 400 to 500 elephants in the whole valley. Maybe less."

Surprisingly, efforts to protect Myanmar's elephants date back to 1879, when the Elephant Preservation Act was enacted to regulate hunting and capture of the species. In 1936 the Burma Wildlife Protection Act prohibited hunting of elephants except by license, and in 1994 the Protection of Wildlife Law completely protected elephants, allowing capture only for scientific purposes. Throughout much of Myanmar, however, such laws are largely ignored, and the Forest Department is powerless to act if the illegal actions are sanctioned by local military officials.

Of an estimated 30,000 to 50,000 Asian elephants remaining in the wild, 4,000 to 5,000 of these are thought to reside in Myanmar. Yet as of 1999, while Myanmar had more than 4,000 elephants documented in captivity, it had no reliable data on wild populations.

The Hukawng Valley clearly still has wild elephants, but no one knows how many. Estimates of 500 individuals left in the valley, as given by the old hunter, might be optimistic. From the amount of fresh wild elephant sign I am seeing, my guess is that the real number is much smaller.

🐾

As I walk along the road one day, trying not to think about the sun beating down on me or the new blister forming on my right big toe, I fill my mind with thoughts of elephants and tigers. No longer paying attention to what's around me, I almost miss what I most want to see.

"Alan, come here." One of the Burmese foresters on our team calls me over. He is kneeling by the side of the road. Sunk in the mud of a shaded wet area is a beautiful male tiger track, six inches long by five and a half inches wide. It had rained the previous night, first a downpour and then a gentle shower. The noon sun has already dried much of the exposed road. There are a few partial tracks in areas nearby that are less soft. The edges of this track are rounded and dulled—the tiger probably had walked by here in the early morning hours.

I find a further patch of mud, one large enough to give me a full set of prints. I measure the tracks again, but now also the distance between them: right front paw to right rear paw, left front paw to left rear paw. The tiger's stride is nearly three feet. That means its body length is close to five feet and its total length perhaps seven to eight feet.

I continue along the road edge until I lose the tracks. Then, on a hunch, I return to the last track I found, which is close to a stream flowing through a culvert under the road. I leave the road and start following the stream into the forest. I hear Saw Tun Khaing say something in Burmese, and two of the team rush to catch up to me. It bothers them when I step off the road, exposing myself to, in their minds, greater danger.

A hundred feet in, the forest opens up as if a small bulldozer had come through. The bulldozer, I realize, was a small group of wild elephants that left their characteristic sign of passing just by walking through the dense jungle greenery. The next partial tiger track I spot tells me that I was correct in my hunch and that the tiger veered to follow the elephant trail. I assumed the tiger wasn't after the elephant, although I knew such encounters weren't unheard of.

Indian-born hunter and conservationist Jim Corbett wrote in his memoirs of two tigers taking on a big tusker in India. And not long before I came to Myanmar I'd heard of an incident in Corbett National Park in India, where a female elephant fought with a tiger that had just killed its baby. Supposedly both animals died in the end. Usually tigers and elephants avoid each other, though. This tiger is simply following the easiest path of travel, I suspect, as big cats tend to do.

I lose the tracks in the matted underbrush, but when the elephant trail crosses another small stream, I follow my gut feeling and turn upstream again. Soon I spot another tiger track in a muddy patch sheltered by a rock on the edge of the stream. Less than a foot in front of the tiger track, tracks of a sambar deer cross from one side to the other. The age of both track sets looks similar, and they seem to have been coming from the same direction. It's possible that the tiger was stalking the deer.

I enjoy this kind of wildlife sleuthing. Even the best hunters consider tracking to be the "fine art" of the sport. You need to know the basics of an animal's habits if you want to interpret sign correctly. Big cats like easy routes of travel such as dirt roads, trails, and waterways. You can even bring a wild cat to an area of your choosing by opening up a new trail.

Once you hit the first good sign, you watch for smaller clues while always looking around you. A depression in the leaves, hard edges to a track, a muddied puddle that has not yet settled out—all tell you that the tiger has recently passed there. A dry streambed, a warning call from a deer, birds suddenly breaking from the trees— each can tell you where the tiger is now. Most of the time you never even get close to the cat, but it's fun to feel as if you are stalking the predator. Every now and then there is a surprise, and you gain new insight into the species' behavior or you come away with more questions than you had before.

There are lots of tracks I find to play with along the stream banks and in the muddy areas of the Ledo Road, and I become more convinced than ever that the Hukawng is one of the best wildlife sites left in the country. But I never expect to actually see a tiger. Not only because of the apparent low tiger numbers and the history of hunting in this area, but also because tigers are so stealthy, especially in large forested landscapes, where they can easily avoid detection. In *Big Game Shooting in Upper Burma*, Major G. P. Evans's observations in 1911 could almost have been written today:

> It is somewhat curious that in the dense, uninhabited forests of Burma, untrodden by man from year's end to year's end . . . both tigers and panthers should so seldom be met with. One would suppose that in such places, where both tigers and leopards abound, they would be met with fairly often in the early morning or evening. But though fresh tracks of both will be found daily, the animals themselves are rarely seen. . . . I do not think this is owing to an instinctive fear of man; for in such out-of-the-way places they have probably never seen a

human being. It would appear rather as if they hid from
the sight of other animals, instinct teaching them that to
make themselves conspicuous in the daytime would
result in them going without a meal at night. That this is
so seems to be borne out by the fact that when either a
tiger or panther is met with in one of these distant spots,
it evinces no fear of man; but boldly stares at the
intruder, eventually quietly taking itself off.

I might have questioned such speculation if not for my own
experience tracking a tiger in the forests of Thailand in the 1990s.
Having followed the animal for more than an hour along a trail, I
lost the its tracks when it veered off into the woods. Turning back
toward camp, I took five steps before lifting my head and seeing,
perhaps thirty feet ahead, a tiger walking toward me. Both startled,
we stopped and looked at each other.

Without any show of fear or aggression, the tiger paused for perhaps fifteen seconds before it turned and walked off into the forest.
I continued back along the trail, studying the animal's fresh tracks.
Not only had the tiger been behind me for a while, but the tracks
and track patterns of this tiger were identical to the tiger I'd been
following. The tiger I thought I was stalking was, in fact, stalking me!

We continue along the Ledo Road to Shinbweyan, meaning
"the place of bamboo shoots" in the Kachin language, a small village of about 500 permanent residents and a couple of thousand
transient gold miners. This sleepy town, the last outpost for another
forty miles before the Indian border, was once a thriving trading
post used by jade and opium smugglers. With the Naga Hills as a
backdrop, I think it the most scenic village along the Ledo Road so
far. A large airstrip cut out of the jungle, overgrown but still intact,
and a small paved piece of road in front of what must have been the
military motor pool are the only signs that this was once a staging
area for American forces coming back over the mountains to fight
the Japanese. A year previously, a tiger was seen on the old airstrip.

After it killed a domestic buffalo, the owner poisoned the carcass. No tigers were seen again in the vicinity.

We rest two days here, staying at the home of the town secretary and planning the next phase, the trip into the rugged terrain of the Naga Hills. Only a few old men still live in Shinbweyan who were around when the Ledo Road was built fifty-five years previously. They say I am the first American they have seen since the war. We are told by the secretary that there is fighting between Myanmar troops and Naga insurgents at Pangsaung Pass, the border crossing into India, and we have to wait for permission from Tanai to proceed farther. The permission comes in short order, but now we are told to proceed only as far as the next sizable village, Namyun, thirty miles ahead, where we will need to wait for further authorization.

The last evening in Shinbweyan, Than Myint and I walk the darkened dirt paths of the town. We pass by the flickering lantern light of a noodle shop, and a customer inside calls Than Myint over.

"Two Naga men came down the mountain today and spoke of a tiger that came into their village, scaring everyone," he says, slurping up noodles as he speaks. Somehow this stranger knows exactly why I am here.

"Where is the village?" I ask.

"About a week's walk from here. Not far. Near the border," he answers, as if talking about a little jaunt.

"Did anyone try to kill it?" I ask.

The man shakes his head. "I don't think so. The Naga said they didn't know who it was."

"*Who* it was?" I repeat, looking at Than Myint inquisitively. Perhaps he has misunderstood or mistranslated. Than Myint questions him further in Burmese, then turns to me with a queer expression on his face.

"I was not mistaken," Than Myint says. Then, standing together in this little noodle shop in Shinbweyan, he relates the story of the Naga were-tigers.

Than Myint and I walk back to the guest house in silence, with only the sound of our footsteps heard along the now quiet, darkened road. I look to the silhouettes of the looming mountains in the distance. I wouldn't understand the context of what Than Myint had just told me until later, once I was in the Naga Hills. But he had fired my imagination.

"What a strange place." I say into the darkness. "What a great place for tigers."

❧ CHAPTER 4 ❧

Into the Naga Hills

From Shinbweyan the Ledo Road winds 100 miles north into the Patkai Mountains to the Pangsaung Pass, then crosses into India. Credit for the construction of this most difficult section of the road is attributed to Lieutenant General Raymond Wheeler, an army engineer working around the clock with Indian contract labor and one of the war's only battalions of black American soldiers. Starting from India and working their way through the mountainous jungles of Myanmar, Chinese soldiers assigned to the road-building crew stayed in front of the engineers and laborers pushing back the Japanese army.

We make a decision to save time by leaving the road and cutting straight up and across the Tawang Bum mountain range. Meanwhile, the elephants will stay on the road and meet us at our camp farther on. We start off in a slight rain that soon becomes a downpour. Though we all slide back in the mud half the distance of each step, we still make better time.

After seven miles we make camp on the ridge. We have new porters and cooks now, having lost our Naga boys and Kachin girls at Shinbweyan. We now also have several soldiers accompanying us, armed with mortar and machine guns, ostensibly protecting us from potential Naga insurgents.

I put my pack down and signal to Saw Tun Khaing that I'm going into the woods for a few minutes. The morning breakfast of salted pork and rice has not been sitting well. I grab the toilet paper and my special pointed stick. The toilet paper is a luxury I refuse to give up since the alternative is the local method of cleaning oneself by scraping with slivers of bamboo. The pointed stick is my weapon against the leeches that start to converge as soon as I stand or squat too long in one place.

It's amazing what men talk openly about when they are camping together in the woods for any period of time. That night around the fire, part of our conversation goes like this:

"Where did you take a crap last night?" Than Myint asks.

"I found a nice spot not too far from camp," I respond.

"I'm holding mine until the next village," says Saw Tun Khaing.

"My system gets totally messed up if I hold it in for one day," chimes in our orchid specialist, U Saw Lwin.

"My ass got bitten to shreds yesterday while I was trying to keep away the leeches. Can the men build us an enclosed toilet area at the next camp?" I ask.

"Everyone in camp has loose stool," Saw Tun Khaing replies. "I think it's better to find your own place."

The next day, after putting on our wet clothes, we hike another eight miles up the mountain to a site designated as Camp 21 by the military. Under other circumstances, I would have immensely enjoyed this hike through the lush greenery and up onto the occasional rock outcrops where the forest opens up and you can gaze at distant mountains. But the constant rains that soak us and the mud that cakes our legs make much of the walk sheer drudgery.

The young soldiers with us seem intrigued by everything I do. They watch me unabashedly as I unpack or undress. They comment on my hairy chest, then point at pieces of equipment that I have: an inflatable sleeping pad, a little coffeemaker, my portable Global

Positioning System (GPS) unit. They seem mystified when I unpack a dead lizard I'd picked up during my hike. I share my secret stash of energy-boosting lozenges with them, then poke fun at their own hairless chests. Most of the soldiers I've met are like this—nice young men who have been fast-tracked through childhood, given few alternatives in life other than the military.

～

MANY OF US ARE NOW WALKING bowlegged because of the irritation in our groins. The tube of Vaseline I brought for my own use was used up within hours when I made the altruistic mistake of sharing it with others. By the end of the day the team is spread out over several miles, each person walking at his own pace. Talk is kept to a minimum. Only after we reach camp, start a fire, and change into dry clothes does any semblance of camaraderie resume.

Evenings in camp are always pleasurable. As elsewhere, people find their own space or seek the company of those they choose to be around. I am always in a group of the four most senior people. We are given the best corners of the huts, the best places around the fire, the first cups of tea, and the best of the food rations. While none of us cares about such niceties, we accept them as a sign of respect.

Our botanist, Saw Lwin, unpacks his tools and plant press and spends a few hours identifying, measuring, and recording the orchids he's collected that day. The ornithologist, U Thein Aung, goes through his field guide, checking on the calls or color patterns of birds he isn't familiar with. I transcribe the notes I took that day from a small waterproof notepad into my field journal. Then I add my thoughts and feelings for the day. Saw Tun Khaing, who usually sets up his sleeping bag near me, writes in his diary.

One by one we finish our self-appointed tasks and wander to the fire. Everyone brings at least one piece of clothing that he wants dry for the next morning. For me it is always my underwear. Most of the clothes I'd brought were swept downriver while being washed by a local girl in Tanai. But trips like this always show me how little clothing and other gear I really need anyway.

I put my bare feet in front of me, close to the fire, making sure that this part of my body stays as dry and healthy as possible. Saw Lwin breaks out his stash of Johnnie Walker scotch that we mix with a little hot water for a version of hot toddies. As everyone breaks into Burmese, I sit back in the darkness and watch their faces.

When you cannot understand a language, you listen with your eyes, the way a blind man sees with his ears. I watch body language and facial expressions, putting words and meanings to subtle movements. I had lots of practice as a severe stutterer when I was a child. Since attempts at speaking were agonizing and often humiliating, I lived in silence most of the time. Now, as then, I prefer to watch people rather than listen to their words. Their intent, I think, is then clearer to me.

The Burmese language sounds unlike anything else I've heard in my travels through Asia. Part of the Sino-Tibetan group of languages spoken by about 21 million people in Myanmar, it is similar to other Indian and Southeast Asian languages in being tonal yet having a syllabic alphabet. The Burmese script developed from the Mon script, which itself was adapted from southern Indian script during the eighth century. The rounded appearance of the letters, called *ca-lonh* or "round script," has been described by some Westerners familiar with video games as akin to Pac-Men fighting. There's a pragmatic reason for such writing, though: When palm leaves were used as paper, straight written lines tore the palm leaves while gentle curved lines did not.

Burmese is one of nearly 3,000 languages in the world, down from more than 10,000 several centuries ago, and it's by no means the only one spoken in this country. Even as we move through just the Hukawng Valley, I'm exposed to a potpourri of languages: Kachin, Shan, Lisu, and Naga, in addition to Burmese. To add to the mix, different villages of the same ethnic group sometimes speak in quite different dialects. Even with a working knowledge of Burmese, I wouldn't be able to communicate with many people living in the countryside.

In the Hukawng Valley, as elsewhere in Myanmar, I am at the mercy of translators for all my information. I have worked long enough with both Saw Tun Khaing and Than Myint so that they know I wish to hear *exactly* what the other person is saying, with as little interpretation as possible. Of course, this is no easy task when the meaning behind a Burmese word or phrase is not easily translatable into English. And it becomes more complicated when I must go through two, or on occasion three, translators in order to get answers to my questions.

I use photographs when asking about tigers or other animals and try to phrase questions so that they can be answered yes or no. Even in one's own language, different names are used for the same animal. The greatest challenge comes when I ask about feelings or emotions. Even the questions can be perceived and interpreted differently by the translator. If an answer to a particular question is very important to me, I will ask the question four or five times in different ways, as trying as this may be for my translator and interviewee, and even me.

We can never fully understand the hearts and minds of people, I've learned after decades of travel and work in remote areas, unless we can speak directly to them in their own language so that the implications, not just the words, come through clearly. Foreign policy actions taken by different governments can be seriously misguided due to a lack of understanding of another country's language. In *Native Tongues*, Charles Berlitz even claims that Hiroshima and Nagasaki might have been spared the atom bomb if a single Japanese word, *mokusatsu*, had been translated differently. Before dropping the bomb, the United States warned the Japanese of a highly destructive new weapon and gave them the chance to surrender before their cities were destroyed. Japan announced that pending cabinet discussion, it was following a policy of *mokusatsu*, which can mean either "ignore," "withhold comment," or "have no comment." The verb was translated by America as "ignore," and the bomb was dropped.

⋙

ON THE THIRD DAY since we entered the mountains, the terrain levels out for a few miles before we descend into a small valley. When I am not focusing on placing one foot in front of the other, I try to discern floristic changes around us as we move from tropical semi-evergreen forest in the valley to the subtropical flora of the foothills. During a rest break, Saw Lwin explains to me what makes the flora in these hills unique, coming as it does from four different countries: India, China, Malaysia, and Myanmar. Unfortunately, in the direction we're going, not much forest is left except on the Myanmar side, he says. Deforestation, population growth, and extensive hunting have created a depauperate wasteland throughout much of the Naga homeland on the Indian side of the border.

We hike fifteen miles, coming within sight of the 900-person village of Namyun by late afternoon. Everyone is worn down. The first thing that catches my eye as we descend the mountain is a military headquarters, and when we get to the village we find two soldiers waiting at a small river crossing to escort us to the guest house. It seems like strange protocol in the middle of nowhere.

With almost four million people, the 48,000-square-mile Naga homeland was divided between two countries arbitrarily by the British. Much of it ended up in India, but a small area, home to nearly 100,000 Naga, went to Myanmar. Since the 1950s, the population in India has struggled for an independent Nagaland that would comprise all traditional Naga lands. While much of the fighting has been in India, regular skirmishes between the Myanmar military and armed Naga insurgents of the National Socialist Council of Nagaland are not uncommon. In Namyun, with only forty miles and numerous Naga settlements between us and the Indian border, the small military force stationed up here is clearly on edge.

Dr. Seagrave, whose book I picked up in the Bangkok book-shop and who was with General Stilwell in the Hukawng during World War II, described the Naga Hills as "no more Burma than they were the valleys of the moon." The abrupt change in topography once we left Shinbweyan and climbed out of the valley bottom, and the ruggedness that I believe Seagrave was referring to, is explained by the relative youth of these mountains, formed when the Indian subcontinental tectonic plate thrust up beneath the Eurasian tectonic plate some 50 million years ago to create the Himalayas. This region is still the epicenter of many earthquakes. But I find myself wondering if Seagrave meant something more by his words. I can feel a tangible difference being in these mountains that seems to have nothing to do with the landscape itself. I feel I've stepped through a portal into a different world.

This is the far northern range of the Naga, also considered good tiger country, with Namyun an important center of Naga culture and trade in the region. These are people notorious for warfare and headhunting, who once kept their smoked heads hanging like coconuts from the rafters of their huts. That was stopped decades ago. Still, I'm a little disappointed not to see semi-clothed natives walking around with full body tattoos, spears, and ornate headwear.

The term *Naga* itself is deceptive, since it was never a name the people gave themselves. Some claim the term comes from either the Burmese word *Na-Ka*, meaning people with pierced earlobes, or the Assamese word *noga*, meaning naked. Regardless of origin, this single name for such a seemingly disparate group of people, with more than thirty different tonal dialects among them, has probably helped shape their cultural identity as they struggle against the governments of India and Myanmar.

After Great Britain granted independence to India and Burma

in 1947 and 1948, respectively, the Indian government made administrative inroads into Naga territory, while the communist military junta that ruled Burma at the time left the Naga to their own devices. Interestingly, the Naga in the Hukawng were best known for their practice of human sacrifice, as a substitute for headhunting. The victims were often children purchased or kidnapped from the lowlands, drugged, and then speared or decapitated. Their blood was sprinkled on the paddy field and their limbs were placed throughout the village. Such cases were documented by the British in the Hukawng through the 1920s, with some reports claiming that the practice continued as late as the 1950s.

One of my objectives for coming into these mountains, apart from looking for tigers and other wildlife, is to continue my search for the leaf deer, called *phet gyi* in Burmese, the new species I discovered in 1997 during my first expedition in the hills around Naung Maung village, north of Putao. Since that time, genetic analysis done by my wife and Dr. George Amato of the American Museum of Natural History has shown this species to be the most primitive deer in the world, with characteristics shown by no other living deer species. Additional morphological and behavioral data I collected from the field all pointed to this diminutive little deer, standing about two feet tall at the shoulder, as a living fossil, with its origins in northern Myanmar. I suspect that this animal's predilection for mountainous topography might take it also into the Naga Hills.

The captain commanding the military installation at Namyun has stayed out of sight since our arrival, apparently reluctant to meet a foreigner. His lieutenant, however, is extremely hospitable and welcomes our company. He puts us up in his house and helps with arrangements for further travel. I explain my desire to interview local Naga about tigers and other wildlife and to travel farther into the mountains to look for the little leaf deer.

SIX NAGA HUNTERS stand before me, having come from two villages ten miles north of Namyun. They've been summoned by the lieutenant.

"We don't go far from our village anymore," one hunter says. "We mostly work our fields."

"No tigers around us now," another hunter from the village farther away chips in. "Only the old people talk about killing tigers. Said they used to take their cattle. Some were shot with old flint guns. Some were caught with steel snares made from the cable used for bridges on the Ledo Road."

"What do you hunt, then?" I ask. They talk among themselves.

"Some animals are still plentiful," one hunter replies. Then they point to the pictures I spread before them: wild pig, macaque, barking deer, sambar deer, pheasant, and jungle fowl.

"What about elephants?" I ask.

"Maybe five years ago we saw elephant tracks regularly. Now no more. They are deeper in the jungle, with the tiger and the bears."

I pull out a leaf deer skull from my backpack, then lay a photograph of the entire animal next to it. The picture is from my second expedition to Naung Maung in 1998, when I paid hunters for capturing a live leaf deer instead of killing it. We brought two of the animals back to the Yangon Zoo.

Four of the hunters have never been far from their village and don't recognize the deer. But the facial expressions of the older two hunters as they converse tell me instantly that they know this animal.

"Not around here," one of the older hunters finally says, picking up the skull and turning it over in his hands. The Naga, like the Lisu, prize such trophies.

"Up there." He points to the distant mountains. The other hunter shakes his head affirmatively. He knows of some villages with these heads, he says. I ask how far away the villages are, and the lieutenant says about fifty miles.

"How long will it take you to go into the mountains and bring me back the hunters and the heads?" I ask. "I will pay you well for your efforts, and I will pay the hunters who come back with you. If he brings me *phet gyi* heads, I will pay everyone extra."

Saw Tun Khaing gives me an admonishing look, as he always does when I promise more money than he believes is necessary. But he translates my offer to the young Naga man who, in turn, translates to the hunters. The Naga hesitate until the lieutenant intervenes, speaking rapidly. The Naga nod their agreement.

"Two, maybe three days." The first hunter now speaks again, but he asks to get paid in rice instead of money. We had had the same request from some of our porters. Now I understand about the large areas of bamboo that I saw broken and dead as we were hiking. A recent mass flowering by the bamboo produced so many seeds that it resulted in a surge of the rodent population. The abundance of rodents, in turn, destroyed much of the villages' rice for the year.

The second Naga hunter agrees to the deal, although less enthusiastically.

"Okay, two days," I say, wondering if he planned to run up and down the mountain. "We will wait."

Over the next few days I wander Namyun, interviewing whomever I can corner. The Naga are reluctant to speak with me, maybe because two armed soldiers are always at my side. Several villagers confirm that there are tigers in the mountains but give no additional details. Some are clearly hesitant to speak openly about tigers, though they speak easily of other animals.

I end up spending much of my time with the soldiers in camp, who travel the area more than many of the local people. Two of the soldiers have recently seen tigers along the Ledo Road, about five miles north of Shinbweyan. One of them saw two tigers together. My best informant turns out to be the head monk, who has been living in Namyun's Buddhist monastery for eleven years. He hears of two or three tigers killed a year by Naga or Lisu, he says, with one particular hunter claiming ten tiger kills in the last five years near the India border. The good news, he says, is that tigers still roam this area. The bad news, I tell him, is that the tigers may be getting killed faster than they are replacing themselves.

The next day the lieutenant allows us to take a short excursion, three miles up a steep, nearby mountain, to reach a Naga village called Cheng Hlaing. With no established trail in place, we hike line of sight, pulling ourselves up the mountainside from tree to tree. I am a bit more watchful about where I step now. The cobra, krait, and Russell's viper—the big three of the poisonous snakes—are all recorded from the Naga Hills.

Cheng Hlaing is fully exposed on the mountaintop. The forest disappears well before we reach the village, the result of continual slash-and-burn agriculture on slopes that have no chance to regenerate. I smell the pigs as we reach the edge of the cluster of about twenty-five houses, in which nearly 300 people live. It reminds me of the Hmong settlements I'd visited high in the Annamite Mountains between Lao PDR and Vietnam—dirty and unsanitary, and located on cold, bare, mist-enshrouded mountaintops far from other villages.

All the houses are thatched and built on stilts, with a terrace in front. The arduous trek required to reach Naga villages is purposeful, originally prompted by frequent intertribal warfare and head-hunting. The hilltops are good vantage points from which to detect attacks, and their climate is considered healthier than that of the lowlands. Most Naga believe that if they stay in the lowlands too long, they will get sick and die.

As protocol requires, we call at the headman's house first. I climb the notched log that serves as steps up to the terrace. As I crouch to enter the doorway, my head bangs into something that sways and clanks like a wind chime. I glance up, and a collection of skulls tied together through the eye orbits swings back into my face. Suddenly, one of the skulls breaks loose and starts to drop, just as I grab it. Thinking I had just had my first contact with decapitated human heads, I step back quickly and almost fall off the bamboo platform.

Saw Tun Khaing laughs. The heads are monkey skulls, used in the past to represent beheaded enemies.

I hold the skull I grabbed at arm's length, realizing immediately that it is the head of a Hoolock's gibbon, not a monkey. Disembodied and stripped of hair, the skull looks strikingly like that of a human child. I can see why some indigenous people won't hunt gibbons, and why the Naga consider this kind of skull to symbolize a human head.

Mention the words "chimpanzee," "gorilla," or "orangutan," and almost anyone can conjure up an image of the animal in their head. But talk about the siamang, the Eastern black-crested gibbon, the Javan silvery gibbon, or any of the other nine gibbon species known throughout the world, and most people look befuddled. Yet this "lesser ape," so-called because of its smaller size, is the most monogamous of primates (including humans), with a genetic makeup only 4 percent different from that of human beings. These acrobatic little primates with their round heads, long arms, and short, slender bodies, swinging through the forests of Southeast Asia, are perhaps the least-known apes on the planet. They are also some of the most endangered.

The headman sits cross-legged waiting for us. We are in one large, open room with a central fireplace, and reed mats have been placed around it for us to sit on. Off to the side is a second, smaller room, where I can hear women's voices. The house is bare of any kind of furnishings, as are so many others I have visited in remote areas. Above the hearth a bamboo rack hangs from the ceiling, with a few baskets on top. Several animal skulls are hung along the wall. Everything in the house is blackened with soot. There are no windows in a Naga house and no ventilation. Always I hear hacking coughs somewhere in the village. Pneumonia and tuberculosis are rife among these people, just as we had been told.

We wait as word is sent around the village for the available men to come and talk with me. When the room is full, I accept a cup of tea from the headman. Then I nod to Saw Tun Khaing, and we start our questions.

The Naga are good hunters, though most of their time and energy is spent working slash-and-burn fields of paddy, maize, and millet. In addition to hunting with crossbows and black powder rifles, they use spears to run down and kill wild pigs. Every part of the animal is eaten, they say, even the skin. But with certain animals, the kill becomes more important than just providing food. The qualities and powers of the animal pass on to the hunter, and parts of these animals become powerful adornments or trophies for the house as well.

When I ask about traditional beliefs of the past, the men become more animated. I learn how the killing of certain species has been important for fertility and social status. In building a chief's house in the past, a sacrifice was necessary, ideally of a human, but at least of a tiger. Today, dogs are sometimes used. One man tells me how the future can be read from animal intestines, or from the way a cock turns its legs when strangled. Another explains that animal sacrifices are sometimes needed to appease the spirits and gods.

Of all the animals, tigers occupy the most special place in Naga lore and culture. One prevalent story of human origin tells of man, spirit, and tiger, all born of the same primal mother. A race is held to determine who gets to live in the villages and who roams the jungle. Man is clever, uniting with the spirit, and shoots an arrow toward the finish line, which crosses it while the tiger is still running. Thereafter, the tiger must live in the jungle.

The killing of a tiger is considered tantamount to the taking of a human head and raises the status of the hunter, who then might adorn himself with tiger teeth and claw ornaments, both considered powerful amulets. If people are quarreling, the chief of the village might have people swear by tiger teeth, or they might be forced to bite a tiger tooth with the understanding that if either lies, the tiger will kill them.

While some of the traditional practices are no longer common among the Naga, their fear of the spirit world and their reluctance to speak about tigers remain strong. Sometimes a hunter will not admit to killing a tiger in case the spirit of the tiger should find out. In some tribes, after a tiger or leopard is killed, a stick will be wedged into the animal's mouth so that it cannot tell the spirits who killed it. Sometimes the dead tiger's ears are sewn shut so that it cannot hear its relatives calling.

Certain Naga, particularly in the days before conversion of the groups to Christianity, were considered powerful seers and prophets, able to converse with the ruling spirits and even roam the forests as a were-tiger. Thus, to a Naga, a tiger is not always what it seems. It may be a were-tiger that has taken one of several forms: the tiger may be the man himself, it may be the man's double, it may be occupied by the man's soul, which left his sleeping body, or it may just be a messenger with a close bond to the powerful human controlling it. In every case, however, the bond between man and tiger is so close that if the tiger is wounded or killed, the seer will develop the same wounds as the tiger, or will die himself within a few days. Few hunters wish to chance killing such an animal.

Some modern Naga, trying to resolve the conflict between the Christian beliefs that missionaries taught them and their traditional animistic beliefs, have modified ideas about the spirit world and were-tigers into a form of ancestor worship. Certain tigers, it is now believed, might still contain the spirits of those long passed. One Naga villager tells me that they respect the tiger because, in times of conflict, the tiger leads them away from people to safe areas. I think the Naga intuitively understand that tigers try to avoid people and their conflicts, surviving best in areas of few people and abundant prey. What better way to escape the horrid conflicts during World War II than to follow the tracks of the tiger deeper into the jungle?

We stay in the village most of the day, knowing that we can

make it back downhill to Namyun in a fraction of the time it took us to get up here. After our visit with the headman, the other Naga open their homes to us. It is a peaceful village, but I see little of the proud, strong Naga people that I have heard and read so much about. These are simply villagers in a harsh land trying to survive.

As we prepare to leave, the headman presents me with a Naga spear that he saw me admiring in his hut, while his wife gives me a belt made of cowrie shells for my wife. I struggle to think what I can give the headman. We brought as little with us as possible for just a one-day trip. Suddenly I remember what the headman was admiring while I sat in his hut. Walking up to him, I take off my favorite Nike cap and place it on the chief's head.

On the trip back to Namyun, I amuse myself and the rest of the team by pretending I am chasing a pig with the spear. As we reach the base of the mountain, I'm surprised to see soldiers waiting for us at the trailhead to the village. After a quick exchange between Saw Tun Khaing and the soldiers, I learn that the lieutenant is in trouble for letting us go into Naga country without an armed escort. The captain, who had been hiding out at the monastery this whole time, has been terrified that something would happen to us and he would be held accountable. His fear has even brought him down from the temple to meet us.

"You are a foreigner and a guest in our country," he says as soon as we meet. "Nothing can happen to you."

I apologize and act contrite, realizing he could care less about my personal welfare.

"It was very important for us to get information from that village," I say. "They were very nice people and we were very safe."

"When I hear you are with the Naga alone, I pray to Buddha," he says, as if I hadn't spoken. "When my men tell me you are safe, I light incense for the Buddha." He smiles, as if it were his prayers that kept us safe.

When the admonition is finished, he returns to the monastery. I never see him again.

Once back in camp, I look closely at the beautiful belt of cowrie shells that the headman's wife gave me. I am fascinated by the presence of such shells in these remote mountains, thousands of miles from their likely origin in the Indian Ocean or Bay of Bengal. Cowrie shells are one of the earliest forms of currency, thought to have been first used as such by the Chinese. The image of the cowrie as a type of currency was so prevalent in many places that the first oval metal coin minted by the Greeks, around 670 BC, was modeled after the cowrie shell. By the eighteenth century an estimated 400 million cowries were being traded annually for the purchase of black slaves, and by the nineteenth, it could take up to 100,000 cowries to buy a young wife. Still, despite such wide circulation, it seems strange to encounter one so far from its origin.

That afternoon, one of the two hunters sent after the leaf deer returns from his mission.

"The old man who knows these deer could not come down the mountain fast enough with me," the visitor says, referring to the second hunter. "He is from Namli village. He tried to come, but I told him to go back home. He says these deer are common in the mountains." Then he pulls from his pouch three leaf deer skulls.

"He also asked if you want this." The Naga opens his hand. Three tiger claws are in his palm, dried blood at the base of one. "He said they killed the tiger last year."

⚬

THE RAINS ARE COMING HARD NOW, and the road beyond Namyun is in terrible shape. Though I would like to go on to the India border, I need new permission from Tanai and the trip would be difficult. More importantly, I feel I have seen enough to make a case to the Forest Department for protecting at least part of this valley. I have seen no other areas of this size anywhere in Asia in such pristine condition and with much of its wildlife seemingly intact. Most importantly, despite the hunting pressures, there are still tigers here.

I encounter no resistance to the idea of our team's returning to Tanai.

The lieutenant suggests that, instead of walking the entire way back, we arrange for boats in Shinbweyan and return to Tanai by river. Because of the river's course, doing so would be a chance to get farther into the interior and see new country. Also, we won't have to slosh through mud eight hours a day and can let our blisters and other skin irritations heal. His only concern, he states offhandedly, is how fast the water is rising from the rains. I thank him profusely for his help and apologize for getting him into trouble with the captain. He requests only that I bring him a fountain pen and ink on my next visit.

In Shinbweyan we rent two long, narrow wooden boats with Chinese engines. Within a few minutes of setting off, I question our decision. The water is muddy and the current fast, and all kinds of debris from upriver, including whole trees, whiz by us. We start off on smaller tributaries, making our way then to the main branch of the Tanai River, which will take us directly to the town. But as the smaller rivers merge, the water becomes faster and more treacherous.

We hug the bank, averaging four to five miles an hour going against the current. Within two hours one of the engines stalls, causing the boat I'm in to drift downstream quickly as the skipper tries to start it again. Saw Lwin looks frightened. He tells me he can't swim.

Our engine breaks down three more times in the next hour before dying completely. We pull to shore and all pile into the remaining boat. The little skiff is overloaded, sitting deep in the water and chugging along slowly as it gets dark. The skipper seems remarkably unfazed as we barely miss being capsized or crushed by a large tree rushing toward us. We bump one of its larger branches and swerve up on the bank just in time. Finally, eleven hours after starting out, maneuvering by flashlight in pitch-black darkness, we arrive at the village of Daipha and are allowed to sleep at the monastery.

From there, it takes only six more hours the next morning to reach Tanai. In light of the last two weeks, the town no longer appears so strange. It seems the lap of luxury. But not luxurious enough for any of us to want to spend another night here.

During our ride to Myitkyina, we discuss our own feelings about the trip. Saw Tun Khaing and Than Myint agree with me that we must petition the Forest Department to protect the Hukawng Valley. The valley houses the watershed of the Chindwinn River, the country's third-largest waterway and the main branch of the Ayeyarwady River, Myanmar's lifeline. Much of the valley's ecological systems appear intact, and the diversity of habitats is such that, when fully inventoried, it might well have the highest species richness of any area in mainland Southeast Asia. Not to mention the fact that Myanmar desperately needs more protection for its tigers.

At the Forest Department in Yangon, I spend days with our field team doing what I love most after being in the field, poring over maps of places I have gone or have yet to go. This time the whole of the Hukawng Valley is spread before me. We banter with each other, trying to decide how much we can ask for and where exactly to draw the boundary lines for a proposed Hukawng Valley Wildlife Sanctuary. The decision is difficult given the expansive landscape and the mosaic of habitats present: natural grasslands, wetlands, closed tropical forest, montane forest.

In the end, we agree on a 2,500-square-mile uninhabited area north of Tanai—nearly a third of the valley, including some of the forest we had just boated through. I draw a line delineating the proposed sanctuary, using the mountains and rivers as natural topographic boundaries. Containing mostly closed-canopy forest, the proposed area encompasses the main watershed of the Chindwinn up to 11,000 feet. It's the largest protected area I've ever proposed. And it has tigers and elephants.

With insufficient time, funds, and people to inventory and protect everything that most needs saving, tigers are my proxy for a relatively healthy environment. Because they are the top carnivore, requiring large areas and an abundant prey base, a healthy tiger population usually means a mostly intact, healthy forest system. As such, tigers are an ideal conservation "umbrella species" and provide good justification for protecting extensive wild areas.

I write the proposal for the new wildlife sanctuary myself, and Saw Tun Khaing submits it to the director-general of the Forest Department. From there, if and when approved, it goes directly to the minister of forestry. Saw Tun Khaing and Than Myint are excited. They are convinced that the Forest Department will expedite our request, even on the heels of the department's recent declaration of the Mount Hkakabo Razi Himalayan region as the country's largest national park.

I am in better favor than ever with the government, they tell me. In August, the *New York Times* published a two-page color spread titled "Indiana Jones Meets His Match in Burma Rabinowitz," detailing our explorations in Myanmar, the discovery of new species, and our efforts to protect this remote region of the Himalayas. The government was thrilled at the good press.

～

TWO MONTHS LATER, while back in the United States, I receive news that U Uga, the director of wildlife, who'd supported our conservation efforts and helped me navigate the government bureaucracy since my first visit to Myanmar in 1993, has been transferred out of his post. Feeling disrespected and unappreciated, he then retires at the end of the year. His deputy director, U Khin Maung Zaw, moves into his position and immediately becomes my primary contact.

U Khin Maung Zaw and I are friends already. He was one of the Forest Department members on the Mount Hkakabo Razi expedition two years earlier, and we had grown close during our months together. While not yet an ardent conservationist, he is a knowledgeable and capable forester who shows genuine interest in our activities.

In the months that follow, while getting reports from some of our trained wildlife teams in the field and waiting to hear from the minister's office about our proposal, I become increasingly concerned, almost desperate, about Myanmar's tiger population. After five years in the country, I now know that tigers are not doing well in most areas. They are already gone from the Putao area and Tamanthi Wildlife Sanctuary, both former tiger sites north and south of the Hukawng Valley, respectively. That tigers are still in the Hukawng is a gift, an anomaly borne of historical events and geographical isolation. But even there, the lower than expected frequency of tiger sign and sightings indicates that the situation is worsening. If we do not get the proposed wildlife sanctuary approved, the Hukawng will soon be added to the growing list of "empty forests"—areas of seemingly good habitat with most or all of their large wildlife gone—that now exist throughout much of Asia.

Into the 1800s, tigers were so numerous in lower Myanmar that they posed a threat to people. Some early Burmese kings adopted the title Sin Kyar Shin—Lord of the Elephant and Tiger. During the 1920s at least two tigers were killed wandering the streets of the capital, Rangoon, one close to the Shwedagon Pagoda. Between 1933 and 1936, with a bounty now on their heads, government records showed at least 1,100 tigers killed, with the actual number undoubtedly much higher. In his book *Elephant Bill*, published in 1950, Lieutenant Colonel J. H. Williams describes Burma as having "too many tigers and leopards in the jungle—so many, indeed, that the few which are shot make scarcely any impression on their numbers."

But at the dawn of the 1960s, Burma was deep in political turmoil and wildlife protection was almost nonexistent. Most ethnic minorities were in open rebellion against the government when General Ne Win seized power in 1962, nationalized industry, and put the country on what he termed the "Burmese Road to Social-ism." By the mid-1970s, Burma had been reduced from one of Southeast Asia's richest countries to one of the world's poorest. Despite totalitarian rule in the cities, rebel groups controlled the countryside and the lucrative border trade in opium, heroin, jade, rubies, and timber. It was open season on wildlife in the forests. Whatever was of greatest value in the Asian markets was exploited the most. Tigers were in everyone's gun sights.

By 1981, based on historical records, the Forest Department claimed that Myanmar nevertheless still had the second-largest population of tigers outside of India, estimating 3,000 tigers in the country. In 1996, shortly after my arrival, the government drafted a National Tiger Action Plan for the minister of forestry, General Chit Swe, who was invited to attend the Global Tiger Forum in India. The Forest Department revised its population estimate to between 600 and 1,000 tigers for the country, based on estimated tiger densities in Thailand and the presumption that tigers occupied much of the still existing available habitat. Their mistake here was in not asking the people who lived in the relevant forests and not looking in the forests themselves. Most people living in the tiger habitat had not seen tigers or tiger sign for a very long time.

My own initial realization that the world's tiger population was likely in dire straits occurred while I was radio-collaring and study-ing Asiatic leopards in a remote jungle area of Thailand in the 1980s. I spent the better part of a year surveying that country's largest protected areas, once famous for the size of their tiger pop-ulation. The results were the same everywhere: many anecdotes, a lot of speculation, but very little tiger sign. A close colleague, Dr. Ullas Karanth, was conducting similar investigations in India while reevaluating his country's accepted tiger census techniques. By the early 1990s we both had reached the same conclusion: the accepted estimates of the numbers of tigers in the wild, somewhere between 5,000 and 7,000 individuals, had to be wrong. The largest cat in the world, roaming the forests for 1.5 million years, was in steep decline and was already gone from many places where it was still thought to be present.

In 1998, before entering the Hukawng Valley for the first time, I published a scientific paper on the status of the tiger in northern Myanmar, describing how tigers had disappeared from many areas where they had once been present. As a result, the Forest Department asked me to help draft a new National Tiger Action Plan. I readily agreed, and requested permission to bring over Dr. Tony Lynam, a wildlife biologist whom I'd hired to coordinate the WCS Thailand Program.

Along with Forest Department staff, Tony and I organized an intensive course in wildlife research and survey techniques, then hand-picked thirty rangers from around the country to attend. The top rangers were appointed to a National Tiger Survey Team, which would spend three years estimating Myanmar's tiger numbers throughout the best remaining forest areas of the country. I offered to take the lead in the Hukawng Valley, still a big unknown area at that time.

The training course for selecting the National Tiger Survey Team was held in the 620 square miles of deciduous forest of Alaungdaw Kathapa National Park, about 150 miles northwest of Mandalay, across the Chindwinn River. Containing a famous Buddhist shrine, this is one of Myanmar's first protected areas; its chief, years earlier, had been Saw Tun Khaing himself. Not long before our arrival there, a British team of scientists surveyed the park and claimed to have found evidence of tigers. I had no reason to question their findings, since Saw Tun Khaing assured me that tigers had once been numerous in this area. The Forest Department, anxious to show that they were doing something for tiger conservation, was considering declaring this park the country's first tiger reserve. It was indeed fortuitous that three of the park staff who were with the British team attended our training course.

"This is what we've done," the park warden says, laying out five plaster of paris casts on a table in front of me. We are taking a break in our 1998 training course after I've just finished a lecture about casting animal tracks. I examine the quality of the casts, then turn them over to read the identifications on the back.

"Who did these?" I ask.

"The British scientists showed us how to do it," says one of the staff. "We made them, and they identified the tracks."

"Are there any other casts that were made?" I ask, reading the backs again.

"Yes, but these are the only ones from cats," he responds.

I call Tony over and show him the casts, then flip them so he can read the identifications on the back. He looks mystified. The two larger track imprints are identified as tigers; the three smaller tracks are labeled as leopards. Anyone who has ever trailed, measured, and observed real tiger tracks in the field would immediately see what I was seeing.

None of the tracks were from tigers. The larger tracks were from Asiatic leopard, and the smaller tracks were likely from clouded leopard or the Asian golden cat. While I wasn't happy about what I had to tell the Forest Department, I couldn't have devised a better training lesson for our course participants.

Subsequent surveys by our tiger team and park staff over the next two years indicated that tigers had been completely extirpated from the park, probably within the past two decades. Assumptions about tigers still being in the park, poor interview data from local people who had no recent experience with tigers, and misidentification of tracks because of insufficient experience—all of these factors combined to produce a completely erroneous conclusion and a potentially embarrassing error for the Forest Department. Myanmar had almost created its first tiger reserve with no tigers in it!

CHAPTER 5

Rolling the Dice

I AM EXERCISING IN MY CABIN, a small, 400-square-foot structure set off in the woods away from our house north of New York City, when my wife, Salisa, comes to get me. It's only 7:30 a.m. She never disturbs me this early.

"It's Myanmar on the phone," she says, sticking her head in the door. "Saw Tun Khaing says it's important."

I walk to the house quickly, sweat dripping off me from the punching bag routine I'd just finished. Unexpected calls from Myanmar are never good news.

"The minister just signed it," Saw Tun Khaing says. He is excited, and I know he's smiling.

I look at my watch. April 3, 2001. It is 8 p.m. Myanmar time. This isn't unusual: the ministers often work late into the night.

"We now have the Hukawng Valley Wildlife Sanctuary," he continues. "The whole thing. They approved the full 2,500 square miles we mapped out. Almost twice the size of our Hkakabo Razi National Park. What do you think?"

"When Hkakabo Razi was signed by the minister, you only faxed me the news," I taunt him, smiling.

"Well, this one is almost two times bigger. It deserves a phone call," he counters.

I am standing in a pool of sweat savoring the rush. In the two years since we drew the lines on the map of the Hukawng Valley I have waited for this, worrying that it would never happen. I bothered Saw Tun Khaing constantly to push the government to sign the documents. The process was slow, he kept telling me. Others beside the minister have to sign off on such a proposal. Eventually he started sending back terse replies saying he could push no more. But now it had happened!

An all-encompassing, you-made-a-difference-in-life feeling sweeps over me. This is only the fifth time I've had such a feeling in twenty years of work, the most recent with the signing of Hkakabo Razi National Park. It's difficult to explain this feeling to people who haven't experienced it themselves. I'm not sure I understand it myself. But it's what drives me, especially when things are at their most difficult.

"Go home now, Saw Tun Khaing," I say, knowing that he's at the Forest Department with his friends. "Thanks so much for staying late and letting me know."

"One more thing," he says. "The director-general wants you to come to Yangon so he can congratulate you. Maybe next month."

I hesitate a moment. This is a strange request.

"The DG wants me to fly 2,000 miles to congratulate me?" I ask. "What's that about?" Saw Tun Khaing and the DG, the country's director-general of the Forest Department, are former classmates and close friends.

"I really don't know. I asked, but he wouldn't say. Something is on his mind. Khin Maung Zaw wants a private meeting with you also, he says. But he wouldn't say why either."

"My visa is still good," I reply. "I'll book a ticket today."

I AM DRIVEN to a local open-air restaurant near the Forest Department called Kon Myint Tha, meaning "Pleasant Higher Ground" in English, a favorite of the staff. It has been raining hard all day, and now it just feels oppressively humid. There are no other patrons, and the restaurant staff hovers around us with umbrellas in case the rain starts again. Saw Tun Khaing, Than Myint, and I are ushered to an outdoor table on the grass where Director of Wildlife Khin Maung Zaw and one of his deputies are already waiting. Seeing me, Khin Maung Zaw immediately orders beer and fried eel, knowing exactly what I like from our previous times together. I sidestep a puddle near the table. As soon as I sit down, the mosquitoes start attacking my sandaled feet.

Something is up. I can see it in Khin Maung Zaw's face. But Burmese etiquette means that serious talk has to wait until later. Right now I am content to drink my beer, chew my eel, and relish being back in Myanmar despite the rain. Over the next few days I plan to meet with government officials to discuss a management plan for the new wildlife sanctuary and pay a courtesy call on the minister of forestry to thank him for all his help with our conservation efforts. I am also looking for the right time to speak privately with Saw Tun Khaing and Than Myint. The last eight years in Myanmar have been the best professional run of my life. I feel it's time for me to move on, though. All I have been waiting for is the designation of the wildlife sanctuary.

In the last two years, Khin Maung Zaw has grown into the job as director of wildlife beautifully. What I first mistook for apathy was, in fact, his careful way of dealing with the political machinations that constantly surround him in the Forest Department. As much as U Uga, his predecessor, had helped get WCS started in Myanmar, Khin Maung Zaw turned out to be an even more forceful voice for conservation. And had I ever doubted his sincerity, I never would again after this night.

Most of dinner is filled with small talk. When the table is cleared and the dessert tray of mixed fruits arrives, Khin Maung Zaw leans back in his chair and starts cleaning his teeth with a toothpick.

"I've read the tiger team report," he says.

After three hard years, the National Tiger Survey Team, formed after our training course in 1998, had finished their tiger surveys. We were still working on the final Tiger Action Plan, but all the data were in. After thousands of camera-trap nights, hundreds of interviews with local hunters, and intensive searching for tiger sign inside seventeen of the nation's largest tiger habitats, tigers were found in only a few areas of the country. Interestingly, much of the other wildlife fauna was still intact in these areas. As I'd suspected, tigers everywhere were being targeted by hunters. Myanmar was facing a much worse situation for tigers than anyone, including me, had imagined. A brief statement to this effect had been sent to the Forest Department before Saw Tun Khaing telephoned me in New York about the news of the wildlife sanctuary.

"It doesn't look good," I say carefully. "Myanmar has far fewer tigers than anyone thought. I knew it was bad but . . ." I slap at another mosquito.

Khin Maung Zaw apologizes to me and then turns to Saw Tun Khaing and Than Myint, speaking rapidly in Burmese. I don't bother trying to discern what they are saying; I'll know soon enough. But when the conversation does finally get back to me, I am astounded.

"Here's the thing, Alan," Khin Maung Zaw starts out. "Myanmar could lose all of its tigers very soon, am I right?"

"Yes, it's possible," I say.

"How could it get this bad?" His tone is almost accusatory. "You recommended the new Hukawng Wildlife Sanctuary because of its tigers. How many are in there? Is that the best place left in the country for tigers? Will it save them?"

The questions are coming fast. And I have no satisfactory answers for him. He flings his toothpick to the ground.

"We don't really know how many tigers are in the sanctuary," I say. "We just know they're there. The team has to do more detailed surveys. But given our findings so far, I believe more than ever that the Hukawng Valley is perhaps Myanmar's best tiger area left."

"So?" he says, spreading his hands as if the rest is obvious. Saw Tun Khaing is expressionless. He clearly knows what is coming but I don't.

"Why not ask the government to protect the entire valley?" Khin Maung Zaw continues. "Why are we protecting only a small piece in the middle? Why not make all of the Hukawng Valley a tiger reserve?" he asks.

I sit there, stunned. Never before have I had a conversation like this with a government official. Never before have I been accused of asking a government to protect *too little* of an area.

"U Khin Maung Zaw," I say in a measured, formal tone. "The government just signed over 2,500 square miles as a wildlife sanctuary. That's almost twice the size of the Hkakabo Razi National Park that we just got two years ago. That's five times the size of the largest protected area Myanmar had before that. That's bigger than many of the protected areas in the world."

I can't believe I am feeling defensive about a situation that, just moments ago, I was savoring as perhaps the biggest accomplishment of my career. At the same time, I try to comprehend the enormity of what the country's director of wildlife is suggesting for me to do.

"The entire Hukawng Valley is nearly 9,000 square miles," I say, thinking as I am speaking. "And there are people in there, tens of thousands of them. With restaurants, churches, schools, shops. . . ." I take a breath. "There is even a prison work camp in there south of Tanai, with about 350 inmates."

"But are there still tigers around these places?" he asks, trumping everything I had just said. I knew there were. And he knew that I knew.

I think back to the many hours we spent deciding on the borders of the wildlife sanctuary, avoiding just such areas that Khin

Maung Zaw now wanted to include. It had been a no-brainer, using the classic paradigm for setting up protected areas around the world: a very large area of nearly circular dimensions, with no people living inside, definable and defensible borders, and seemingly intact habitat and wildlife populations. Because protected lands come at a considerable premium, few scientists ever get the luxury of making such decisions. Usually government bureaucrats decide on the wheres, whats, and hows of a protected area, and in the end, there is rarely enough land set aside for the largest, widest-ranging species. This time, however, I was actually able to set up what I believed was a nearly ideal protected area. And I now found myself being called on the carpet for it.

"Let's expand the wildlife sanctuary," the director of wildlife says emphatically. "Go back to the government. Show them the tiger data. Ask for the whole valley, the whole 9,000 square miles. Tell them it is a necessary part of the Tiger Action Plan."

Saw Tun Khaing remains quiet. I look at him, and he shrugs. We are discussing something on a magnitude that is, to me, almost incomprehensible.

"I don't understand," I say, looking hard at Khin Maung Zaw now. "You are the government! You are the director of wildlife of the Forest Department. You are in charge of protected areas. Why don't you and the director-general simply recommend the expansion of the sanctuary yourself?"

Khin Maung Zaw shakes his head.

"You have been in our country long enough to understand by now. You have the ears of men in power. They all know about you and WCS. And my minister trusts you. He will listen to what you say."

I sit back, speechless. Although flattered by Khin Maung Zaw's words, I am still dubious of the outcome of such a request. More importantly, I am not sure I even want to make it.

I sleep little that night. I had returned to Myanmar thinking that the Hukawng Valley Wildlife Sanctuary was to be my swan song.

Now I am being asked by the Forest Department to push forward a conservation initiative for which there is no precedent in the country, and one that is unlike anything I would have ever considered myself. Even if it is possible, will I now risk the loss of the new wildlife sanctuary by having it absorbed into a much larger, less manageable entity, before the ink is even dry on the documents? Would the Myanmar government consider a new protected area larger than many small countries? Do I want to risk everything?

ALL of the Hukawng Valley as a tiger reserve. I turn the idea over and over again in my head. Right now the valley contains upwards of 50,000 people comprising at least four major ethnic groups, the entire township of Tanai as well as parts of five other townships, and the jungle headquarters of the country's largest insurgent group, the Kachin Independent Army. It seems like lunacy!

I smile. On the other hand, lunacy is a crucial component of real-world conservation. Only those who set goals beyond what is obviously achievable make a real difference in this world. And right now we needed to make a difference in tiger conservation.

For years, biologists who work with large-bodied, highly threatened, wide-ranging species such as big cats, elephants, and birds of prey have known that the traditional paradigm of conservation—setting up hard-boundary, self-contained protected areas—is just not working. We continue to lose many of our most magnificent species because most protected areas are not large enough to encompass viable populations of such species, and because we are unable or unwilling to address the human-wildlife interface outside protected areas. Then we seem surprised when we fail, when the forests are empty of the species we claim to be protecting. Tigers are the poster child for such failures.

Big species need big spaces. The 2,500-square-mile wildlife sanctuary, while perhaps not the optimal habitat for tigers, was a chunk of land big enough for possibly at least 100 tigers to live there and thrive. But the long-term health of any species is dependent, in part, upon genetic exchange between many different individuals or populations of that species. And I was bothered by the fact that some of the best tiger habitat in the Hukawng, the grasslands and wetlands, remained mostly outside the designated sanctuary.

When I set aside all the practical considerations, I realize that the ideal scenario for tigers, elephants, and other species here would be conservation at the largest possible landscape level, with the wildlife sanctuary as a core stronghold within that landscape. The potential tiger population for the whole valley, if protected and managed properly both inside and outside the sanctuary, could be in the range of 400 to 500 tigers. This could be the largest single tiger population in the world.

People must learn to live with wildlife, not apart from it. Conversely, wildlife conservationists must be flexible when it comes to national and local ideas about growth and development. Ultimately, conservation success can be achieved only by the people who live and work in the landscape. While a balance between such interests seems inherently logical and achievable, the real-world implementation of such an idea is so complex that few people or organizations dare to attempt it at the different levels at which it must occur. Working at the national level with government officials is not enough; working on the ground with local communities is not enough; it must all be done together, like fitting the pieces of a jigsaw puzzle in place.

There are few truly large wild landscapes in the world where such ideas can even be tried or implemented. But we are not without some comparable precedents. In northern New York, the third most populated state in the United States, sit the relatively rugged Adirondack Mountains, some of the oldest rock formations in North America. Both Native Americans and early European colonists avoided the area's inhospitable environment until an explosion of resource extraction opened the Adirondacks to settlement in the 1800s. With uncontrolled clearing threatening up to 80 percent of its forests, the Adirondack Park was created in 1892 and expanded over the next century to include a 9,375-square-mile area of public and private lands that now contains at least 150,000 permanent residents and millions of seasonal visitors. Throughout that time, conflict remained a recurrent theme with timbering, mining, tanning factories, and other industries going through boom-and-bust cycles. But always the fundamental idea of balanced preservation persevered, allowing for dynamic cycles of change that included both resource use and renewal. Today the Adirondack Park is considered a rich mix of history, culture, economics, and wilderness with a vast capacity for adaptation and recovery. Many wildlife species once hunted to extinction—moose, peregrine falcon, beaver, the bald eagle—are now thriving and coexisting with people. Why cannot something like this be the future of the Hukawng Valley, I wonder?

However I look at it, Khin Maung Zaw seems to have gotten it right. The Hukawng Valley is a unique opportunity at the right time to model landscape conservation and save tigers on a scale that is unprecedented in this part of the world. How could I not take up such a challenge?

FOUR DAYS LATER, we drive through the Ministry of Forestry complex on Kaba Aye Road in Yangon and park alongside the almost hidden side entrance to Minister U Aung Phone's office. We arrive an hour early and are shown into a private waiting room. On previous occasions, when I still thought logic governed our actions, I questioned why we always needed to be at the minister's office so long before our appointment time. The answer was that if the minister was ready to see us earlier than our appointment, we had to be available on a moment's notice. In eight years, this hasn't happened yet, so I loosen my tie, sip the lukewarm tea in front of me, and settle back to wait.

Just getting entrance to the inner sanctum of any of the offices of the country's thirty-nine ministers is no simple task. Logistically, it is difficult to even pin down their schedules. When not in one of their innumerable meetings, they travel the countryside visiting various projects or accompanying a high military official as window dressing. And when they are in their offices, access often depends upon the ever-shifting political climate between Myanmar and the rest of the world's countries. After the Clinton administration imposed limited sanctions involving new investment in Myanmar in 1997, Americans didn't rank very high on the "should see" list.

Fortunately, as Khin Maung Zaw had said earlier, I was a known entity to the government now. My friendship with the former forestry minister, Lieutenant General Chit Swe, who had recently been forced to retire, still carried me in good stead with the new minister, Aung Phone, his former deputy. While I don't feel the closeness and mutual respect with Minister Aung Phone that I had felt with General Chit Swe, the minister has so far acted favorably on all of my requests, even though conservation is not high on the government's agenda at this time. Still, I am very careful of what I say, how I say it, and what I ask for, though I always push the bar a little higher with each meeting I have. Today I will see just how high the bar will go.

After the initial pleasantries, I review the details of the tiger team's report, explaining that by the end of the month we would have a full Tiger Action Plan to present to the cabinet. I know the government doesn't want to lose all its tigers. But how far will it go to save them?

"So we know tigers are in terrible shape in Myanmar. We could lose them completely in the next few years," I say to the minister.

"The new Hukawng Valley Wildlife Sanctuary that you approved is a very good area for tigers, Minister. That's why it was chosen. I truly thank you for all you have done." I take a deep breath.

"But frankly, I didn't know how bad things were at the time. If I had known, I would have asked for an even larger area to protect." I pause, waiting for a reaction. There is none.

"If we were to protect all of the Hukawng Valley as a tiger reserve, I could possibly increase the number of tigers that would live in the sanctuary by more than three times. I could definitely save the country's tigers from extinction." I look the minister in the eye, and my stomach churns. I can't even fathom the ramifications of my request, much less convince myself yet that such an endeavor can even succeed.

The minister politely apologizes to me, then speaks in Burmese to the various people in the room, particularly his two director-generals from the Department of Forestry and the Department of Planning and Statistics. Khin Maung Zaw is not present. I maintain eye contact with the various parties in the room so as not to lose the moment, while the clock on the wall ticks away the seconds.

In long discussions prior to this meeting, Khin Maung Zaw and Saw Tun Khaing had allayed my initial fears about giving up a sure win (the defensible, hard boundary–protected sanctuary) for a huge long shot (the indefensible multipurpose landscape with tens of thousands of people inside). I learned from them that the easiest and fastest way to protect the valley as a tiger reserve is to create extensions to the existing Hukawng Wildlife Sanctuary in priority areas most important for the tigers.

Of course, there still remained the practical consideration of how we could protect the whole valley when we don't even have adequate staff and resources to protect the core. What the hell am I doing? I suddenly wonder.

At last, Minister Aung Phone turns back to face me.

"We must do whatever we have to in order to save the tigers in my country. The Hukawng Valley is a big place, and there are many other interests there. We will not move any people, and you will have to work with them so that they benefit from this scheme as well," he says.

"Minister, the plan is simple," I say, almost choking on my words. "We already have the wildlife sanctuary in place. This is the most important area. Now we will identify other areas of the valley that are important for tigers and propose them as extensions to the sanctuary." I feel a bit awkward explaining forestry law to the forestry minister.

"With your permission, I would like three years to gather all the information we need to properly structure and manage the new tiger reserve extensions across the valley. The Forest Department will need to settle existing land claims and demarcate community development zones. And I will have more time to make sure that funding is in place for the reserve. Then the new tiger reserve can be declared," I say.

The minister looks at me while I speak. As soon as I finish, he turns and speaks with the director-general of the Forest Department, who nods.

"I will take your proposal to the cabinet. I will explain what you told me regarding what we need to do to save tigers. I am trusting that you can make this happen," he says.

"I will make it happen," I say.

The minister stands, signaling the end of the meeting.

On the ride back to our office, no one speaks for the first ten minutes. I don't know if Saw Tun Khaing is annoyed with me or just shell-shocked at what I have just committed us to.

"I have no idea where to start," I finally say, looking out the window and speaking to no one in particular.

"You made a promise to the minister," Saw Tun Khaing says. He makes it sound as though I have just sold my soul to the devil.

"Don't worry, I'll keep the promise," I say, realizing that all my ideas of packing up and going somewhere else had just vanished. I had at least three more years here to make this work. Not much should change in the valley during that time, I think.

"I'm not worried," I say aloud.

But I was worried. And if I had had any idea of how wrong I was about the changes that would soon come to the Hukawng Valley, I would have been far more worried.

⚐ CHAPTER 6 ⚑

Into the Darkness

"DADDY, GET UP. It's light out." Alexander is shaking me. At twenty months old, with a vocabulary that is growing daily, all he wants to do is talk and play.

I roll off the bed. As I stand, my left leg buckles from a shooting pain in my knee. My joints have been acting up since I returned from Myanmar a little over a month ago. I check the clock: 8 a.m., almost three hours past my normal wake-up time. God, I am feeling old lately. Tired all the time, and now with aching joints. I'll need a lot more energy than this if I am to continue going into the field and be able to keep up with my son too.

Alexander is excited. We are leaving for England. He has no memory of his plane ride across the globe to Thailand at the age of six months, so this seems like the first big trip. The plan is for my wife Salisa, Alex, and me to spend a week in Chester in northwest England, where I will give a lecture on jaguars and discuss a possible joint conservation program with the Chester Zoo. Then I'll return to New York while they go on to visit relatives in the Lake District for another week.

These are happy days for us. After a couple of bad years of miscarriages, bitterness, and marriage counseling, our relationship is

73

going well. Fatherhood has been a blessing I never imagined possible and now, after much discussion, we have decided to let nature take its course to see if we can have a second child.

In the meantime, the work and planning for the Hukawng Valley consumes me. I've asked Than Myint to divert our tiger team and make the Hukawng our top priority for now. Back and forth on e-mail with the field staff, I review maps of the Hukawng Valley, picking potential survey sites to be reconnoitered as protected extensions to the sanctuary as soon as the dry season starts.

The plan is for the field teams to scour the study area, looking for tiger sign. Then, using GPS units to plot exact locations, they will place specially designed camera units at particular sites within a grid system that maximizes the chances of photographing tigers. All sites will have two cameras, each one hooked up to an infrared sensor that triggers the camera when any warm-blooded animal walks in front of it. Since each tiger has a distinctive stripe pattern —its own fingerprint, so to speak—a picture of a tiger taken from both sides will "capture" that individual, allowing us to distinguish it from any other tiger.

Over a six-month dry season, the team will move the cameras several times to photo-trap several hundred square miles of habitat. Analysis of the capture data will allow us to accurately estimate numbers of tigers in those areas sampled. Initially we will focus our efforts on the core wildlife sanctuary. Later, the team will expand to different habitats within the proposed extension areas.

Tony Lynam, who helped me train the National Tiger Survey Team, has agreed to return and work with the tiger teams in the field. Excitement and anticipation have replaced my initial fears. Now that I'm committed to this path, there is no looking back.

I return to New York on September 7 and delve into my work, taking full advantage of an empty house for a week. The book I've been working on for the past year, *Beyond the Last Village*, detailing my early experiences in Myanmar, has now hit the bookstores. All reviews so far are good.

On September 10, Salisa calls from England.

"God, I miss you," I say upon hearing her voice. "The house feels so empty without you and Alex. I'm getting lots done, but there's no one here to make me laugh."

"You never laugh anyway," Salisa says. She believes I have no sense of humor at all. The line goes silent after that. I think we've been disconnected.

"I'm pregnant," she says suddenly. Her tone is neutral, waiting for my reaction. She knows I am ambivalent about a second child. We've had long discussions about how it might affect my work and upset the dynamics of our relationship. But in the end, we both agreed that Alex should have a sibling. We just weren't sure if Salisa would easily get pregnant again, though we were doing nothing to prevent it.

"Are you sure?" I ask, saying the first words that come into my head.

"I'm sure. I missed my period this month. I wasn't going to tell you or do anything about it until I got home. But my sister insisted. She went out and bought the test. What do you think?"

I feel annoyed, even a bit angry. Why did she do the test without me there? Why did she decide to tell me over the phone? What did this mean for my book tour or my next scheduled trip to Myanmar?

"I'm glad," I say. "This is what we talked about. Alex needs a brother or a sister. Just let me get used to it, okay? It would have been nice if you were here in person so I could hug you. Let's talk again tomorrow. I love you."

But tomorrow is September 11, 2001. As I am driving to my office at the Bronx Zoo, New York City is attacked, and the eyes of the world turn toward the gaping void that was once the World Trade Center complex. The second call to Salisa never happens. I can't get through.

Salisa and Alexander are finally able to return to New York a week later than originally scheduled. Despite a world out of balance, Salisa appears quietly content. I am now truly happy about the pregnancy. The events of September 11 only reaffirm my commitment to life, in all its forms. Bringing a child into this world and helping save tigers from extinction are two sides of the same coin.

⁓

"ALAN, WAKE UP." Salisa is hovering over me, looking worried. "You were tossing and moaning. The bed is soaked."

The fatigue and achiness I've been feeling for almost two months now have become much worse in the last week. But this is the first time I've had night sweats. I feel as though someone dumped a bucket of water over me while I was sleeping.

When I'd visited my doctor shortly after returning from England, she thought I might have picked up some viral bug in Asia. Now, when I return to her a month later feeling worse, she checks my blood again. This time she recommends a specialist.

"Please, sit down." Dr. Friedman walks in and motions to a chair. Pictures of smiling children and an attractive wife sit atop the desk, turned at just the right angle for visitors to see. All office pictures look the same, I think. No one's ever ugly, and their lives are always wonderful. The doctor smiles at me. My stomach knots.

"I've gone over your last few blood tests and examined your blood now," he says. "There's a steady rise in white blood cells. The problem is that they're not normal white blood cells. Normal cells are heterogenous. That is, they're different from one another."

"I know what 'heterogenous' means, Doctor," I say. It comes out a bit hard.

"I'm sorry," he responds. The smile is gone.

"The new white blood cells are identical to one another, a condition called monoclonality. The fatigue, aching joints, night sweats—they are all common symptoms at the onset."

"Onset of what, Doctor?" I ask. This is not going well.

"You have either leukemia or lymphoma," he says.

He sits back, gauging my reaction. "I don't know which," he continues. "I advise we do a bone marrow biopsy. Right now, here in the office."

Leukemia, lymphoma, bone marrow biopsy. The words ring in my head like bullets ricocheting to and fro, destroying brain tissue.

It all means the same thing—cancer.

I am taken into one of the clean white rooms with the same cold and impersonal feel of every other clean white room in doctor's offices throughout the country. I am told to wait while they prepare the long biopsy needle that will be inserted into my hip to penetrate my bone marrow. I stand by the window and watch a mallard duck splash around a little man-made pond in a large grassy area beyond the parking lot. Some native cultures believe that ducks bring comfort and protection. Right now, I feel naked and vulnerable. I wonder if I'll ever see the Hukawng Valley again.

I take out my cell phone, start to call Salisa, then hang up. What do I say? "Hi hon, I have cancer. Not sure what kind yet, but don't hold dinner. I've lost my appetite for a while."

I remember a boy in one of my classes in high school who came to school one day looking pale and sick. The word "leukemia" was whispered in the hallways. After a few weeks, he stopped coming to school. He wasn't there the next year.

I open the phone again, then close it again. Finally, I dial my home number.

"Hello?" Her voice sounds happy. I almost hang up.

"It's me. I'm still at the doctor's." My voice breaks a bit.

"Do they know anything yet?" she asks. She hears it in my voice.

"I have cancer," I whisper. My nose and mouth are pressed against the window. I watch the ducks.

I remember two things from that day: the slight sucking sound followed by a burning sensation as they aspirate bone marrow from my hip and, later, the tears welling up in Salisa's eyes, hand resting on her belly, as I explain what the doctor said to me. How many times do we wake from a nightmare grateful that the real world is a better place than the world of our dreams? I couldn't wake up this time.

In the days that follow, I search the voluminous information on the Internet about leukemia and lymphoma. I learn the comforting fact that leukemia is a "malignant neoplasm of blood-forming tissues," sometimes induced in animals by viruses. My mind reels from the acronyms and pathologies describing the variations of leukemia that I would have been happy to go to my grave never knowing about: AML, ALL, ATL, CML, CLL, HCL, SLVL, and myelodysplastic syndromes representing progressive bone marrow failure. Lymphomas are similarly described as "a heterogeneous group of neoplasms arising in the reticuloendothelial and lymphatic systems." But here the list is short: Hodgkin's disease, non-Hodgkin's lymphoma, and mycosis fungoides. The rate of disease progression for this buffet of blood cancers varies from fast to slow; the probability of cure varies from high to none. I go into the room I use as an office, close the door, and turn off the lights. I sit on the floor and put my head in my hands, trying to muffle the sobs.

I return to the doctor a week later, sit down in the same chair, and look at the same family pictures. But this time, Salisa is with me. I wanted to come alone, but she insisted on being there also. Someone needs to listen carefully to what is said, she tells me. She is right, of course.

Dr. Friedman walks in and apologizes for keeping us waiting. How much bad news has he already given out today, I wonder. He wears the same smile.

"I have pretty good news," he says, surprising me.

"You made a mistake. I don't have cancer," I say half jokingly, half hopefully. What other good news could there be?

"No, but you have what I consider the best kind of cancer.

What you have is something called CLL, chronic lymphatic leukemia. . . ."

I hear nothing after the word "leukemia." I remember reading about CLL. The most common form of adult leukemia in the Western world, it often goes undetected until a routine blood examination, like mine, shows something abnormal. But the most important thing I remember is that there is no known cure for it. If it gets bad enough, a bone marrow transplant may be attempted.

". . . early stage . . . nothing to be done now . . . more tests to be run . . . second opinion. . . ." I catch fragments of his words while Salisa jots down notes, listening intently.

"How much time do I have?" I ask the question that every person in my situation must ask.

"That's impossible to say. It's a chronic condition that rarely becomes acute," the doctor says. "Progression of the disease can be very slow, or it can speed up at some point. There are treatments to knock it back, different kinds of chemotherapy, but not until you need them."

"Why not treat me now, when it's still at an early stage and I still feel healthy?" I ask.

"Because you may need the drugs later, and they won't be as effective."

"Okay then, Doctor, just give me an approximation. I need something."

"How old is your son?" he asks. I think he is changing the subject.

"Almost two," I say.

"Don't worry. You'll see him bar mitzvahed," he replies, as if he is giving me good news.

I turn to Salisa. She tips her head a bit to the side and curls her lip, trying to look reassuring. She does that when she tries not to cry.

Eleven years, I think. That's not enough time!

I order whatever books I can find on CLL or leukemia. The list is not that long: *Adult Leukemia: A Comprehensive Guide for Patients and Families; The Official Patient's Sourcebook on Chronic Lymphocytic Leukemia; Surviving Leukemia.* I scour relevant journals such as *Blood, Leukemia*, and *Leukemia and Lymphoma.* I read snippets:

> . . . characterized by progressive accumulation of well-differentiated malignant monoclonal B lymphocytes in blood, lymph nodes, liver, spleen, and marrow. Progression of the disease is typified by increases in blood lymphocyte count; increases in the size of lymph nodes, liver and spleen; and advancing anemia and thrombocytopenia. Although chemotherapy may palliate symptoms, there is no established cure. . . .

> The other way it [CLL] kills you is by interfering with the immune system. It does this either by making the immune system overactive or underreactive. If it becomes overactive it starts attacking your own body rather than just infecting germs, so-called autoimmunity. . . . An underreactive immune system is almost universal in CLL. . . .

> So far there are no treatments that regularly cure patients with CLL. There are patients who have been in remission for a very long time who might be cured, but since we know that some patients have very slowly progressive leukemias we cannot predict the future.

Always, before finishing, I close the books or journals and toss them. Attempts to distance myself from my own emotions fail miserably. This particular cancer is not as well researched as many others. Older books describe CLL as a disease primarily of men over sixty years of age, who have an average life span of ten years after diagnosis. More recent literature gives more hope. But since there is no cure, there is no treatment in the early stages. The doctors all seem to agree: save what's in the medical arsenal for when it's needed. I can't know at this point whether my disease is aggressive or slow, or whether there is a specific genetic defect known from some cases of CLL that could pass to my children.

Day after day I sit in the darkness of my office at home, not knowing what to do next. I'd spent much of my life fighting the world as a stutterer, finally breaking from the dark closet of my childhood to be accepted by people, and finding comfort with animals in remote corners of the world. Then, remarkably, I met Salisa. I married at forty years old, had my first child at forty-five, and now a second child is on the way. There is wonderment and purpose to my life, and it feels great. Now, overnight, all feelings of strength and vigor are gone, as if a plug has been pulled. I feel broken again, defeated.

I don't talk about it with Salisa, and she doesn't push. Why burden her with the pain and sadness I feel inside, I tell myself, as she prepares for the arrival of our next child? I see her also retreat to a safe place inside herself, as she did when we were having marital problems. I resent it a bit, wanting her to break through my walls, wanting so badly to be held and comforted. My mother and father loved me but never knew how to comfort the angry, frustrated child I was. Now my wife, who loves me, doesn't know how to comfort the sad, hurting husband I am.

I know I make it hard for everyone. I push people away, secretly hoping that someone, sometime will push back and break through. Usually I just cry alone in the dark.

For four days I barely leave my room. "Here," Salisa says finally, laying a piece of paper down in front of me. "The doctor gave this to me before we left his office. It's the name of a grief counselor. He thought you might need it. You do need it."

"There is no way . . ." I start to say. Then I see Alexander standing in the doorway, looking scared. He knows something is wrong, but doesn't understand anything. "Okay, thanks," I say, taking the paper. Salisa squeezes my finger.

THE GRIEF COUNSELOR works out of a local church in New York's Westchester County. She is in her fifties, with a gentle, soft-spoken demeanor. I feel fifteen years old again, as if I'm coming into the office of yet another speech therapist or psychologist telling me in a soft, slow, gentle voice that everything will be okay. But none of the therapists who tried to console me ever stuttered, and this nice woman in front of me doesn't have an incurable cancer.

But in spite of myself, I find that it feels good to be with this stranger and let my thoughts and emotions boil over for a while. Then I listen as she tells me of the five stages of grief common to cancer victims: denial, anger, resentment, fear, and sadness. I knew these stages well. I'd already gone through all of them during my tortured years as the boy who couldn't speak, placed in classes for "special needs" children—the "retarded classes," as my classmates called them.

I am certain that I will not go through these stages again. Those doors have closed behind me. I feel I have already dealt with more denial, anger, resentment, and fear than most people ever have to in life. No, this time I'd skipped right to the sadness—that deep, pitch-black hole of sadness that arises from the thought of not seeing one's children grow to adulthood.

I let Salisa tell people close to us what is happening, since I have suddenly shut myself off from everyone. One of my good friends, Jane Alexander, actress and former head of the National Endowment of the Arts under President Clinton, comes to see me. She knows the president of Memorial Sloan-Kettering Cancer Center in New York City and has arranged an immediate appointment for me with the chief of hematologic oncology.

The entrance is on Sixty-seventh Street between York and First Avenue, and I park five blocks away. My briefcase is filled with pathology slides, radiology films, and blood test reports that will now be handed over to the new doctor. On Sixty-fifth Street I linger at a Dunkin Donuts sipping coffee, not wanting to go closer, not wanting people to think that I am one of "them," another can-

Into the jungles of the Hukawng Valley on the search for tigers.

Early gold mine traffic on the newly opened Ledo Road, Winter 2002.

Stuck along the Ledo Road after a day's rain.

Typical bridge crossing built by local people to reopen the Ledo Road.

Forest with tiger sign inside the newly designated Hukawng Wildlife Sanctuary.

Expanse of natural grasslands in Hukawng Valley.

*S*urvey team setting up camera traps near a fresh tiger pugmark
in Hukawng Valley. Three camera trap photos of tigers. Survey team in our office in
Yangon identifying individual tigers from their distinctive stripe patterns.

Camera trap photos taken along a walking trail inside the sanctuary.
Lisu hunter with (top to bottom) wild boar, clouded leopard, sambar deer,
and Asian wild dog (dhole).

Asiatic leopard cub orphaned when hunters in Hukawng Valley killed its mother to sell her body parts for use in traditional medicine.

Young Lisu boy proudly displaying his father's trophies: sambar deer antlers and a piece of a tiger's jaw.

KIA soldiers patrolling their own administered territory inside Hukawng Valley.

Daw Khin Htay (far left), leader of our socio-economic team, explains the new hunting regulations for the valley. Her assistant sits on the far right.

Shaman from a remote Naga village maintains some of the old ways,
adorned with a tiger skin hat, cowrie bead bracelet, and a necklace with beads
of amber and parts of animal jaws.

cer victim, another damaged, broken person not as good as everyone else. How familiar these feelings are to me. All those years of
not speaking, of having no friends as a child, so I could pretend I
was like everyone else. So that no one would know my mouth was
broken.

I finally make it to the front doors, go in quickly, and head
straight for the A-bank of elevators in front of the coffee cart area,
as I was instructed over the phone. I avoid eye contact. With my
briefcase, maybe people will think I'm a doctor. The doors open at
the fourth floor, and I go to Suite 440. The ruse ends.

As soon as he walks into the examination room, shakes my hand
as a colleague, and starts talking science, I like Dr. Stephen Nimer
immediately. We are of similar age, we are both research scientists,
and we each "googled" the other before this meeting. With nearly
200 scientific publications under his belt, Dr. Nimer is one of the
top leukemia researchers in the field, specializing in bone marrow
transplants. While I was in the field following jaguars and tigers, trying to save them from extinction, he was in the lab struggling to
understand leukemia. What we share is a deep, abiding passion for
our work, a love of science, and a strong desire to save lives—for
him, those of humans, for me, those of animals. We connect
instantly.

After an almost cursory examination of the materials I have
brought in, Dr. Nimer confirms the diagnosis of Dr. Friedman.
Then he examines me, feeling the lymph nodes under my arms and
in my groin and palpating my spleen. Without missing a beat, he
delves into the etiology of leukemia and where the latest research is
heading, as if we had just met at a scientific conference.

"Look, Alan. I can go over each of the blood numbers with you
in detail, but it doesn't necessarily mean much. I'd like to see you
every month for a while and check your blood. We can use the
white blood cell count as a gross indicator of the rate of progression. In the end, though, all that matters is how you feel and how
your body is responding. You're in the earliest stages of this disease.

So much research is going on. I mean it when I say, try not to worry about it. You'll be around a long time. I'll make sure of it." Nimer glances at his watch, then apologizes. He has to leave and see other patients. At the door, he turns.

"One last thing, Alan." He smiles. "I tell people in your situation to just go about their life as normal. But your life is not normal, and I have a feeling you'll do what you want to do no matter what I say. In many ways, that's the best thing. But there is one caveat. There is a possibility, though by no means a certainty, that any contracted illness could kick your immune system into high gear and speed up this disease. I see from your chart that you've had your share of parasites and diseases from the places you've been. Be more careful. Take more precautions. I'll see you next month."

My steps are lighter as I leave his office than when I had walked in. But his last words stay with me. The elevator stops at the third floor and a bald little girl, no more than ten years old, is wheeled on with a bag of fluid running into her arm. We glance at each other, but she looks away quickly. She is embarrassed, just as I was when I walked into the building. But her life hasn't even started.

"Don't let my disease be passed to my children," I pray silently to a God I don't believe in.

CHAPTER 7

Letting Go

On Dec 31, 2001, my forty-seventh birthday passes quietly. A scheduled trip back to Myanmar to survey Hponkan Razi, a mountainous area north of the Hukawng Valley that I thought should be protected, is cancelled. Instead, Dr. George Schaller, my mentor and friend, who has worked for years in Tibet and India and was to go on the expedition with me, agrees to go alone.

I am at a loss about what to do with my life now. I can stay in New York and administer projects from my office at the Bronx Zoo, be more careful with my health, and perhaps guarantee a few more years with my family. Or I can go back into the field, pursue the challenges and visit the places that I've come to love so much, but spend less time with my family and perhaps shorten my life.

More than eight months have passed since I made my vow to the minister of forestry on establishing the tiger reserve: "I will make it happen." Despite our great staff in Myanmar, they can't undertake this massive endeavor without outside help. Nor can I orchestrate the creation of the new Hukawng Valley Tiger Reserve from an office in New York. The problem weighs heavily on me. But I am as uncertain of my next step in life as I have ever been.

I have always loved traveling—the butterflies in my stomach

85

when arriving at a new place, the challenges to be met, the new sights and smells, the fascination of learning about different cultures. I used to travel to run away from a life I felt I wanted to leave behind. Now I travel to feel complete, to feel as if I am moving toward the person I want to be.

"The sole cause of man's unhappiness is that he does not know how to stay quietly in his room," the French mathematician and physicist Blaise Pascal wrote in his *Pensées*. That's far from my thinking. Rather, I share the view of contemporary British philosopher Alain de Botton, who writes in *The Art of Travel*: "If our lives are dominated by a search for happiness, then perhaps few activities reveal as much about the dynamics of this quest—in all its ardour and paradoxes—than our travels."

In 1790, a twenty-seven-year-old Frenchman, Xavier de Maistre, undertook a journey around his bedroom, later writing about his experiences in a book called *A Journey around My Room*. He followed that up with a second journey in 1798, traveling his room by night and entitling his account *A Nocturnal Expedition around My Room*. De Maistre, who on the surface appears to share Pascal's view, passes off these excursions as suitable for those "who never dared to travel and others who might not be able to." Yet his work has much deeper and more subtle meaning, suggesting that the pleasure we derive from a journey is more dependent on the mind-set we travel with than on the destination we travel to.

Right now my mind is numb, though. Every step I take, be it around my room or outside the front door, is filled with uncertainty. I am scared.

In May 2002, my beautiful little daughter is born. Her godparents, Jane Alexander and Ed Sherin, are by Salisa's side, assisting with the birth every step of the way. At five pounds and three ounces, she comes out with a head of shiny black hair like her mother. Her name, Salisa and I agree after long discussions, will be Alana Jane Rabinowitz. The Jane is for her godmother. The Alana is for me. It is Salisa, still unsure of how long my time might be with her, who suggests that we give our daughter my name. It is a gift from the heart.

I would never have imagined that such a joyous event could be tinged with such deep sadness. I stop going to the office because word has gotten around that I have leukemia and people are acting contrite toward me, as if they've done something wrong. I stop exercising for the first time in thirty years, and I give away my weight-lifting equipment. There seems no point to any of it now. One of my wife's favorites among my T-shirt collection, emblazoned with "Eat right, exercise, die anyway," now stays in the drawer. I won't answer the phone, not wanting to hear sadness or pity in anyone's voice. I cancel a second trip to Myanmar, still scared of moving forward.

I feel so empty inside that I am immobile. Despite the urging of others, I refuse to see any more counselors or therapists. Instead, I start studying tai chi with David Yee, an accomplished martial artist and acupuncturist who lives nearby. I feel uncomfortable attending classes with others, so twice a week he meets me privately at his studio and we practice until about 10 p.m. The tai chi exercises comfort me, as does David himself. Having had a difficult childhood also, David empathizes with my struggle but shows no pity. He brings back the fighter in me.

❦

"ALAN RABINOWITZ . . . most mysterious great cat . . . put his life on the line. . . ."

I walk into the living room one morning and see my image on the television. Alex sits on Salisa's lap, watching intensely.

"Daddy, look. It's you. You're saving jaguars again," Alex cries, his voice filled with excitement.

"Who put this on?" I ask Salisa.

"Alex picked it up from the VCR rack and put it in. He thought it was his cartoons. Once he saw you, he wanted to watch it. Which one is this?" Salisa asks. "I don't remember seeing this footage before."

"It's from that series called *Champions of the Wild*, three years ago," I say. "Don't you remember when I had to go back to Belize? They used footage from when I first worked there, then filmed my return twenty years after setting up the jaguar preserve."

I stand there watching with them, seeing the young, strong body of the twenty-six-year-old Alan Rabinowitz catching jaguars and putting radio collars on them when no one thought I could do it. Then I listen to my own voice from just a few years ago, older, more experienced, but with the same surety of purpose:

"There were many times when I thought I couldn't finish it. I felt that, emotionally, I just can't go on. But I did, because there was no other choice."

I look over and see the faces of my wife and son. My son turns to me.

"Can I do that too, Daddy? Can I go with you and help you save animals when I get a little bigger?"

Salisa is looking at me.

One afternoon when I was fifteen years old, I stopped by the store to pick up my mother's groceries on the way home from school. When it was my turn at the counter, I couldn't say my last name. Pointing to the bag, I felt my head and shoulder start twitching as I tried to get my name out. The young woman at the counter mistook me for a mentally handicapped person and apologized to the people waiting behind me, who were murmuring impatiently. Willing to do anything to escape the ridicule, I accentuated my spasms, distracting everyone by purposely knocking over someone else's food items. Then I grabbed my own bag and ran from the store. I felt sick to my stomach at how I had demeaned myself, and swore I would never again let anyone dictate who I was and what I could do.

As I watch my son's face, that same feeling of self-loathing surfaces within me. Can I really break this easily again? Will I deny my son the person I've worked so hard to become, and the father I want him to know?

"You can come with me, Alex," I say. "You can come with me whenever you want. There will be lots of chances. I promise."

The next morning I wake up before sunrise as usual. Instead of getting out of bed, I snuggle up against my wife's back and kiss her neck. She reacts almost instantly, reaching over and moving her hand to my thigh. We haven't touched for months.

"It's okay now," I whisper.

She murmurs something I don't understand. Her hand continues to wander.

"I'm going back to Myanmar," I say.

She turns to face me now, fully understanding the implications of what I am saying. She hugs me, and I sink my face into her hair as my eyes mist.

"Can you wait until after breakfast?" she asks.

CHAPTER 8

Hungry Ghosts

With distant snow-covered mountains to my back, I stand at a podium in the cool midmorning light of Putao in November 2002, facing nearly a hundred people dressed in colorful ethnic garb. Though the purpose of my trip lay in the Hukawng Valley, I've agreed to a slight diversion. The occasion is the opening of a new environmental education center built by WCS. This spacious 2,100-square-foot concrete building, costing a little more than $10,000, consists of a large exhibit room filled mostly with photographs and specimens from our recent expeditions, and two smaller rooms—one a natural history library, the other a movie room with TV, DVD, and VCR to show nature films.

Erected a little distance away from the building is a small, open wooden structure housing more than fifty orchid species from the region. This is the sole environmental education center in northern Myanmar, and only the third in the country. The people of this frontier outpost have never seen anything like it. It is my organization's gift to them and a tribute to Mount Hkakabo Razi National Park, the 1,500-square-mile Himalayan protected area signed into law by the government in November 1998.

I finish my speech to polite applause, then cut the ribbon strung across the front door. Lisu, Rawang, and Kachin young people mix freely with town officials and military officers, pointing at skins or stuffed specimens, laughing at photographs, and looking in awe at parts of animals that many of the attendees have never seen or did not even know existed. I think of all the questions I get back in the United States about why I am in Myanmar. Since the publication of *Beyond the Last Village*, my work in this country has become much better known. But the statements of certain political groups and news articles about my efforts have not always been favorable. A number of Burmese activists say openly that no one should engage with this military regime, regardless of the reasons. I wish my critics could see the faces of these people now. If wildlife conservation has first to be considered through political filters, then where should I work in the world? And when did animals get to vote and decide what governments they must live or die under?

While the primary purpose of my work is to conserve wildlife and wild habitats, I would be courting failure if I did not consider the lives and livelihoods of the local people who live with that wildlife. If any conservation effort is to be sustainable, the people most affected must view themselves as its beneficiaries, not its victims. This does not mean that when there are human-wildlife or land use conflicts, people should always get their way. It means that for the most important human issues—education, health, and food security—positive improvements made to people's lives should be linked to the protected area or to other conservation efforts that affect them. While compromise is a necessary element of conservation, the benefits must outweigh the negatives for the majority of both the people and the wildlife.

❧

"THIS IS STILL COLD," the monk says. "Put it in the sun for a day, then put it out under a full moon. Rub it between your hands as much as you can. It will help you. Just never let it touch the ground. It will lose all its power." The small silver ball that U Einda Sara, head monk at the Buddhist monastery in Putao, places in my hand is only about half an inch in diameter, but it is extraordinarily heavy for its size.

"He gave you a very special gift," Saw Tun Khaing says as we leave the monastery. "It took him a long time to make that ball."

"Did you tell him I was sick, Saw Tun Khaing?" I ask.

"I told him your doctors say that something is wrong with your blood and that they cannot help you," Saw Tun Khaing says. "Our people don't think that way."

I understand the value of this gift. I had seen Einda Sara palming this ball, or one like it, in his hand every time I visited the monastery in Putao. The first time I'd asked about it was when I learned of this monk's practice of alchemy. He explained to me how these balls were made, by pouring acid over one tikal (half an ounce) of silver and one tikal of brass. Water was added to neutralize the acid, and then one tikal of mercury was mixed with the ash to make it pliable. Finally, citrus juice was used to remove the ash. Then the mixture was rolled continuously by hand until it became a ball. Eventually the ball could turn to gold, Einda Sara believed. But his objective was not to make gold for its value, he said. It was to create a powerful spiritual object for meditation and healing. I grip the ball tightly.

Since my return to Myanmar, Saw Tun Khaing is on a mission to cure my leukemia. He cannot believe that I can appear so healthy while some insidious illness slowly destroys my body. After years in this country, I am still learning about the complexity and depth of beliefs that lie just below the surface of this predominantly Buddhist culture. Whether in Yangon or in the farther reaches of the northern hills, offerings are made to *nats*, or spirits. There is still strong belief in the evil eye, seers, astrology, magic, and necromancy. People commonly wear amulets, and some still practice alchemy, exorcisms, and divinations. A Burmese teacher at the International School in Yangon tells me of his belief that the Hukawng Valley is the residence of Buddhist *wezas*, or wizards. Saw Tun Khaing claims to believe in none of this, yet he prefers local, traditional concoctions to Western medicine, and he does not discount the power of the monk's magic ball.

Saw Tun Khaing even arranges a meeting for me with U Min Thein Kha, the famous Seer of Myanmar. This sixty-seven-year-old chain-smoking author, astrologer, and former political prisoner resides at a sprawling Buddhist commune in Hmawbie, about a two-hour drive from Yangon. Hundreds of Burmese, including numerous high-ranking military officers, arrive at his compound daily seeking advice and predictions.

Dressed in loose-fitting clothing, cigarette in hand, Min Thein Kha walks into the little room where I have been told to wait. Sporting a mustache, a goatee, and long, unkempt wavy black hair, he reminds me of an old hippie from the '60s. Except for his piercing gaze. He seats himself before me, smiles, and then starts turning over tarot cards. When all the cards are laid down, he ponders for a few minutes, then speaks with Saw Tun Khaing.

"He has a lot to tell you," Saw Tun Khaing says to me. "But he does not want to lose the meaning in words. He will write it all down for you, and I will translate it. Overall, though, he says your life looks good, but there will always be unrest and struggle."

"What about my illness?" I ask. Saw Tun Khaing turns and speaks with him.

Min Thein Kha turns his gaze on me again and scans my body slowly. He looks at the cards, then at me again, shaking his head just slightly.

"He says he sees no illness. Perhaps it is too early. But your body and spirit are strong. If something comes and tries to take over, you will persevere," Saw Tun Khaing says.

❧

FROM PUTAO I FLY BACK DOWN to Myitkyina, where a truck is waiting to take us again into the Hukawng. Now that I'm committed to setting up the entire valley as a tiger reserve, I need to get my feet back on the ground again and develop a clear strategy for how we proceed. Only now, three and a half years after my initial visit, everything is different. The truck belongs to us, just purchased by WCS for the new wildlife sanctuary, and behind the wheel sits U Myint Maung, the newly appointed chief of the sanctuary. Myint Maung is an old friend. He was our top trainee in the tiger training course in Alaungdaw Kathapa National Park and was subsequently appointed co-leader of the tiger survey team. When the surveys were completed, most of these well-trained, jungle-hardened Forest Department staff were sent to help manage some of the country's badly neglected protected areas. At our request, Myint Maung was assigned to the Hukawng Valley Wildlife Sanctuary, the country's newest and largest protected area.

As we drive toward Tanai, Myint Maung catches me up on events that have happened since we were last together in 1998. Then we discuss my conversations with his boss, Khin Maung Zaw, and the minister of forestry in Yangon nearly a year and a half earlier. His already difficult job is now much harder as we move forward on two fronts—securing the core wildlife sanctuary and assessing the potential of the rest of the valley as extension protected areas. When and if it is all brought together, I point out, he will have the entire Hukawng Valley Tiger Reserve, 2 percent of the country of Myanmar, to manage.

Myint Maung remains quiet after I stop talking. I turn my gaze out the window while he concentrates on maneuvering along the road. The mountains in the distance tell me that we are just entering the valley. Myint Maung finally speaks again. His lack of practice with English causes him to hesitate, searching for the right words.

"A lot has changed in the Hukawng since you first went in," he says.

"I'm sure some things have changed. Three and a half years brings changes to even the most remote areas."

"You will see," he says again. Then he turns to Than Myint and speaks with him in Burmese for the rest of the drive. I am left to my own thoughts.

﹏

As WE DRIVE INTO TANAI, my first impression is of a town strikingly larger, more crowded, and much noisier than before. But what I am not prepared for at all suddenly looms large in my vision. The drivable road no longer ends at the water: a 942-foot iron bridge, completed just nine months earlier, now spans the Tanai River.

At the same time that the cabinet was approving the wildlife sanctuary, and the minister of forestry was agreeing to the idea of protecting the whole valley as a tiger reserve, other government departments, with no communication among them, were hard at work rebuilding the washed-out bridges that had kept the valley isolated for decades. The reason given for fixing a road that went nowhere, and for sudden attention to an area that had been off everyone's radar for decades, was rural development. But the deeper reason, I soon learned, had to do with an element that triggers human fantasies and greed more than any other: gold.

While the presence of gold in the Hukawng Valley had been known for over a hundred years, gold extraction was always a small-scale local activity. Until recently, the exploitation of this resource had been restricted to individual gold panning by local villagers wanting additional income. People dug on dry land, on sandbanks along rivers, and even underwater using simple tools such as spades, buckets, iron bars, bamboo sieves, and wooden pans. The remoteness and inaccessibility of the area kept organized, larger-scale gold mining using mechanized equipment from developing in the Hukawng Valley in the way it had developed elsewhere in the Kachin State.

But Tanai Township officials, thinking that more efficient gold extraction could bring increased wealth to the area and to their pockets, had successfully pushed the government to rebuild the bridge that once spanned the river and provided access deep into the valley. This effort was supported by the Ministry of Mines, which, unaware of the activities of the Ministry of Forestry, was expanding its bidding process for prospecting concessions because the gold in other areas of the state was becoming increasingly difficult to mine. The Kachin Independent Army, also seeing an opportunity to fill their coffers, had followed suit, filing a request to develop gold mining operations in their own administered territory within the valley.

Beginning a year earlier, in 2001, advertisements in magazines around the country had urged people to come to the Hukawng Valley and get rich. The ad campaign worked, unleashing a frenzy unlike any the valley had seen before. Although there were only a few sites inside the Hukawng where gold mining of this kind was even practical, that mattered little to the impoverished masses, who were ready to grasp at any opportunity. Within months of the opening of the Tanai bridge, tens of thousands of itinerant laborers had poured into the region with only one thing on their mind: gold. What followed was a major setback for our efforts to protect this valley.

I sit with Saw Tun Khaing, Than Myint, and Myint Maung, listening as they explain the background behind everything I now see going on around me. I am almost numb with shock and frustration. As we sat with Khin Maung Zaw and the minister, as we sat for hours in various vehicles going to and fro, and as we made our way here, no one had thought to tell me anything about what I would be seeing. My only warning came on the way in, from Myint Maung, who stated that a lot had changed in the Hukawng since I'd last been there.

I sit quietly, knowing full well that it will do no good to berate anyone. If I were to ask why I was not told about some of these things before, the reply would be that I never asked. Two decades under a regime that discourages, and sometimes punishes, independent thought and action has clearly had its effect. If I were to make up a credo that depicts much of Burmese behavior as I have experienced it in the country over the years, it would be: "Speak only when spoken to. Answer only what is asked, and even then, be careful what you say."

In fact, in theory, I have no problem with the rebuilding of bridges and the opening of the road. Our plan for the tiger reserve would eventually have recommended such an action in order to provide better access and economic development for local communities. What is devastating is the reaction of entrepreneurs and impoverished people to the sudden opening of a resource-rich area that has been essentially closed for decades and is now, they believe, the answer to all their prayers .

I stay in Tanai only as long as I have to, anxious and also apprehensive about seeing what changes are taking place elsewhere in the valley. But on this journey we waste no time walking. The forty-four-mile section of road from Tanai to Shinbweyan, part of the old Ledo Road, is now a busy, dusty thoroughfare. Amid a constant flow of trucks stacked high with food supplies, gasoline drums, and PVC pipes, I barely recognize places where I had once leisurely meandered, measuring tracks of tigers, elephants, and wild dogs, or spent quiet evenings sharing meals with local villagers. Many new settlements of Lisu and Kachin have sprung up along the route. In places where food had been scarce and rice was a more desired barter item than money, there are now coffee shop huts catering to the traffic and its passengers.

We pass the remains of an old campsite where a bear had growled at us during the night. Farther on, a little oxbow lake where I'd seen several wetland bird species now sits empty. I remember the daily flocks of hornbills and troops of macaques that had burst from the canopy as we passed. Now there are only deeply rutted tire tracks along the road, and the sounds of the forest are drowned out by truck engines.

At each of the two biggest rivers, the Tawang and Taron, barges made from wooden planks straddling motorized longboats charge the exorbitant fee of 10,000 kyats (about US$10) to ferry people and vehicles over to Shinbyiyang, and 5,000 kyats to come back toward Tanai. Some people pay a lesser fee to have their vehicles pulled across the river by local elephants.

On our first expedition we had walked across a shallow section of the Tawang, sinking up to our waists, then arranged a boat to take us over the Taron. Now some vehicles chance the crossings themselves. If they are unlucky enough to get stuck in the loose gravel midriver, they are charged twice the going rate to be rescued by an elephant. Everyone's destination is Shinbweyan, where the biggest and most accessible gold mine is said to be. The desperate hunger for quick riches hangs like a heavy stench in the air.

We reach Shinbweyan in three hours by truck; walking, it had taken us five days during our first trip here. At first, the beautiful hamlet set deep in the valley below the Naga Hills appears unchanged. We go directly to the house of U Ba Sein, a Naga who is the secretary of Shinbweyan. We had camped out on the floor of his house in 1999; now he is the proud owner of a small two-story guest house, complete with a new outhouse in the back. I had fallen through the bamboo floor of his last outhouse. I ask about the changes I see.

"Before, the town had about 600 people, with several thousand gold miners scattered throughout the forest. Now we still have only 680 people in town, but out there . . ." He turns and points in the general direction of the mines. "I don't know, maybe 50,000 gold miners."

I am incredulous as I look in the direction he indicates. I realize, suddenly, that I can't see any tree line.

I walk to where the forest once started at the edge of the village. Now the trees are far in the distance. Before me is a massive open space, perhaps six to seven square miles in size, filled with pits, sluices, and bamboo huts, resembling a shantytown atop a desecrated moonscape. Instead of animal sounds, I hear Burmese karaoke and the constant noise of hydraulic pumps and truck engines. Everywhere I turn, I see high-powered jets of water tearing into the ground, creating slush that is filtered for gold before being dumped.

"Watch your step—don't fall in," says Daw Myin Yang as I step close to the edge of a deep, ugly pit in the ground. This is her gold mine, on land leased from government officials. Ironically, her husband is a local forest guard who has been working with our team to protect the forest.

"See what we got yesterday?" She holds out her hand, proudly displaying a pea-sized ball of glistening gold. It is worth 13,000 kyat, the equivalent of $13, and her final profit, after deducting expenses, will be only a fraction of that. Still, in the economy of modern Myanmar, this is something to be pleased about.

My eyes move from the gold back to the pit, perhaps thirty feet deep. Two mud-covered workers strain to steady a high-powered water hose that is eating away at the earth, making the crater larger and deeper as I watch. At one edge of the pit a woman squats over a large wooden bowl, her hands wrist-deep in pure mercury.

Most of the gold mining in the Hukawng is being done like this, I learn: a family or small group of investors leasing a plot from township officials, then using savings or borrowed money to work the claim. A typical small mining operation starts off with at least three miners, one pump, and one suction dredge. Either on dry land or on slopes along the river, the earth is first blasted with water. As promising sites are identified, certain areas are cleared for test mining. Once gold is actually found, the work at that site begins in earnest. Rocks and wood that can't be sucked out by machine are hauled away manually. As the walls of the mine are hosed down, the muddy earth is collected by the suction dredge and sieved through plastic netting.

The final prize—gold—is separated out using mercury. Gold bonds to mercury, forming a composite known as amalgam that is more dense than the gold itself and thus easier to collect from the sediment. But considerable amounts of mercury are left in the waste of this process, called the tailings—leftover crushed rock and mercury mixed together. The tailings are subsequently dumped into rivers or left at the mine site, where they seep into the ground.

The bonded gold-mercury amalgam is heated with blowtorches or over open fires to burn off the mercury and get the pure gold. In the process, miners and anyone nearby are exposed to toxic mercury vapors. Vapors that are not inhaled settle into the surrounding environment and, along with the tailings, are eventually metabolized by organic matter that transforms the elemental mercury into methylmercury, a powerful neurotoxin. As the methylmercury makes its way up the food chain, it accumulates in fish and wildlife.

As much as 95 percent of all the mercury used in gold mining operations such as this one is released into the environment. Each day of these mines' operation wreaks further havoc on the surroundings and makes the natural recovery of these sites, once they are abandoned, that much less possible.

Saw Tun Khaing taps me on the shoulder and points. A deforested, sterile landscape, pockmarked with pits, stretches into the distance. Some of the pits belong to gold companies and are much larger than the one we stand before, with more people and machinery eating away at the earth. Men covered head to toe in mud, women hauling rocks or huddled over bowls of mercury, children running to and fro, playing and crawling on toxic ground. There seems nothing remotely good or civilized about what I see before me. It is like a scene from nineteenth-century England, when whole families of men, women, and children slaved in factories for fourteen-hour days just to earn enough to stay alive.

We walk along the edge of the clearing for half a mile and enter the ragtag assortment of tarps and ramshackle buildings that house and supply the thousands of people toiling at these mines. Stalls crowded together offer food, coffee, pharmaceuticals, hardware supplies, clothing, haircuts and even massages. Every shop has scales to weigh the gold brought in for barter.

We take seats at a corner stall and order Cokes. A set of legs hangs from a rafter by the kitchen.

"Wild boar," I point out to Saw Tun Khaing. "Tiger food."

"They have fresh sambar deer too," Saw Tun Khaing replies as he reads the sign listing the daily specials in Burmese.

We sip our Cokes without speaking.

"Do you still think we can pull this off?" Saw Tun Khaing asks quietly.

I am asking myself the same thing.

Traditional Buddhism teaches the existence of six levels of the cosmos into which one can be born. Three levels below that of human beings is the pitiful level of the hungry ghosts, *petti-visaya* in Pali. These hungry ghosts are characterized by insatiable desire, depicted by huge bellies and tiny mouths, and their realm is a desecrated, all-but-uninhabitable landscape. All around us now flow rivulets of thick, brown, lifeless water, devoid of life, poisoned with cyanide and mercury. It's the land of the hungry ghosts.

On the walk back to the village, I look beyond the devastation to the distant greenery. Keep perspective, I remind myself. The animals are still out there, I know it. These ugly wounds and the poisons put into the earth are no small matter, but there is still the expansive, untouched forest beyond.

Shinbweyan is not the only area undergoing rapid and destructive change, though. Four other, smaller gold mines have opened elsewhere in the valley, three of them under control of the KIA. Luckily, the 2,500-square-mile wildlife sanctuary was announced before the gold rush and remains officially off-limits to human incursion.

Still, the sudden surge of humanity in all these areas demands enormous resources. Trees are being cut for building materials, and the forest is being scoured for wild game. Guns have replaced crossbows as the weapon of choice, and farmers have become hunters for profit. The meat of sambar deer and wild pig, essential food of tigers, is now cheaper than domestic chicken and pork in the valley, both of which must be trucked in from Myitkyina. Traders are coming in asking after bear paws and bear gall bladders, highly valued items in the Chinese traditional medicine trade. Once-quiet rivers are being dynamited and netted so that almost nothing edible escapes.

Along the banks of the Tawang River I come upon a ragtag assortment of twenty rattan collectors, camped out on the rocks after bringing their latest haul of rattan downriver. They are unemployed Burmese from central Myanmar, the dry zone, brought here for four months to collect as much rattan as they can, from wherever they can. They are paid between 50 and 150 kyat (5 to 15 cents) for every fifteen feet of rattan, depending on the quality of what they collect. This is the second year they've been here, they tell me, and they already have to go eight nights upriver to find good rattan. Once cut, the rattan is floated downriver and stacked in piles to be picked up by truck.

Superficially similar to bamboo, which is used and sold locally as building material, rattan has much greater economic value because of its combination of firmness and pliability. Most of it will end up as furniture or baskets for export. Local villagers in the Hukawng have been harvesting this resource for nearly three decades, cutting about 30 *lak* (1 *lak* = 100,000 pieces) each year and selling it to three companies in Tanai. But now, with road access, more outside labor has been brought in, and harvest rates have increased as much as tenfold. The wild supply, according to one buyer's estimate, is perhaps two years from depletion.

My concern now is what comes next. Some of the people who came for the gold rush are settling, clearing land, and planning to stay. Myanmar Oil and Gas Enterprise is drilling exploration wells in the valley. There is room for both development and conservation in this expansive landscape, I know. But the wrong kind of development, or development sprawling over too much of the landscape before we get a handle on identifying what needs to be protected, could tip the scales against the conservation value of the tiger reserve.

As bad as it all looks right now, the Hukawng Valley still tops my list of places I have seen in the last decade that offer both expansive habitat and the potential for a large tiger population. But with the pressures on the wildlife populations accelerating rapidly, I need to know whether there's a viable tiger population in here now. Can this newly booming Hukawng Valley, where death and destruction have been the status quo for centuries, really be turned into a functional and long-lasting tiger preserve? I need answers soon.

❧ CHAPTER 9 ☙

Where There Be Tigers

WHEN WE RETURN TO TANAI from Shinbweyan, we're met by U Saw Htoo Tha Po, a forty-two-year-old former Forest Department veterinarian, who joined the WCS Myanmar staff five years ago and is, along with Myint Maung, a co-leader of our tiger survey teams. With him is Daw Khin Htay, a forty-year-old woman who leads the socioeconomic team that was formed to gather information about what is happening in the communities outside the wildlife sanctuary. She is an anomaly in the Forest Department: still single, she has managed to break the cultural and bureaucratic barriers that keep most Burmese women from venturing far from the home.

Saw Htoo Tha Po hands me a thick envelope filled with contact sheets containing three months of photographs from the camera traps set up in selected jungle areas of the wildlife sanctuary. This first effort will give a density estimate of tigers inside the core of what we hope will end up to be a much larger tiger reserve. Since the wildlife sanctuary appears to be one of the least disturbed parts of the valley, the size of the tiger population there will help indicate whether or not the larger tiger reserve is even feasible. If a viable breeding population of tigers has not been able to survive in the sanctuary, the chances of finding a larger number of tigers in other parts of the valley are slim.

I walk onto the wooden terrace of our bungalow and squat down to spread the sheets out in front of me. Using a magnifying glass, I go through the photographs. The team mills about nervously, as if waiting to find out the results of their own test scores. I skim the photographs quickly, then start again from the beginning, looking over each picture much more carefully a second and sometimes a third time. I check the dates and times of day for each picture indicated on the film, then note the location coordinates of the camera that took the pictures, written on the top of the contact sheet. Finally I put the sheets back into the envelope. In the course of twenty minutes, I have gotten a peek into the tiger's world that would have taken me months of intensive fieldwork to get on my own. Now I think I better understand what we are dealing with.

"What are the numbers?" I ask, referring to a more detailed analysis of the photos that was done before my arrival.

"We estimate one to two tigers per hundred square miles, maybe twenty-five to fifty in the sanctuary. Maybe eighty to a hundred in the whole valley," Saw Htoo Tha Po replies. Myint Maung concurs.

I turn the numbers over in my mind. Despite the rigor of the methodology for small plots, extrapolating from the density estimate for the sample area to the much larger protected area is a stretch and risks overestimation of tiger numbers. But at least the numbers provide a rough approximation. Cutting them in half would yield a safer, more conservative estimate.

However it's calculated, the tiger density and the estimated numbers of individual tigers in the valley are very low, much lower than what I had hoped for. Some well-protected tiger reserves with similar habitats in parts of India, by comparison, have at least ten times the tiger density we are seeing. But even if we are dealing with only twenty to twenty-five tigers in the core sanctuary and twice that many in the whole valley, we have enough of a population to build upon. If tigers can be protected in the Hukawng Valley so that their numbers are allowed to increase to their full potential given the size of the area, the population could grow to ten times the number of tigers we have now. We could have the single largest number of tigers living within a tiger reserve, which itself would be the world's largest.

But after looking closely at all the photos, it is not the low density of tigers that bothers me the most. Right now I'm wondering how much time we have before recovery of the population is impossible.

"We've got some beautiful tigers in here," I say to Myint Maung, referring to the flash-lit images of the few healthy-looking tigers captured in the photos. "But we've got some serious problems."

Myint Maung looks at me, deadpan.

I pull out the contact sheets again and spread them out. Everyone gathers around.

Apart from the pictures of tigers, there are photographs of thirty-two other species of mammals and birds, indicating an intact natural system, at least for the larger vertebrates. That's the good news. But while all of the photos taken at night show pictures of animals, almost all of the photos taken during the day are pictures of people, walking the same trails as the wildlife. Many of the men in the photos carry crossbows or guns. One man waves and smiles at the camera. Another is carrying a dead monkey. He is wearing a KIA uniform.

"What do you see?" I ask Saw Htoo Tha Po and Myint Maung.

"Animals and people," Saw Htoo Tha Po replies.

"Weapons," Myint Maung adds.

"What else do you see?" I ask, pointing to all the unexposed film that remains on each roll.

"Nothing," I answer myself. This is the worst of the news.

After examining thousands of camera-trap photos from sites around the world, I know what to expect. In places where wildlife is abundant and relatively undisturbed, a roll of thirty-six frames is almost always fully exposed with pictures of animals over a three- to four-week trapping period. Usually there are multiple pictures of the same species, with few pictures of people. The amount of unex- posed film remaining on these rolls indicates diversity without abundance. The pictures of people carrying weapons give the likely reason behind this. Most worrisome is the seeming paucity of the tiger's favorite and necessary foods: sambar deer and wild pig.

Remembering the meat I saw for sale at the food stall in Shinb- weyan, I turn to Khin Htay and ask what they've been finding in their interviews with local villagers. She places a sheet of tabulated data in front of me and starts explaining what she knows.

"Most of the people we've interviewed have been women," she begins. "They run the stalls in the market, and they do the cook- ing. The most common wild animals killed and sold for food, espe- cially near the gold mines, are sambar deer and wild boar. They sell for about 1,000 kyats to more than 1,500 kyats per pound. Barking deer and gaur are also sold, but not so much. And as you know, wild meat is sometimes twice the price of pork and chicken."

"Do you have any idea how many sambar deer and wild boar are being killed?" I ask.

"We don't have that much data yet. Most of our information comes from what the households are buying or consuming, not killing," she says, looking at her data.

"Households at or near the gold mines seem to be consuming an average of 260 to 300 pounds of sambar deer and 30 to 70 pounds of wild boar a year. This is about six times more than what an average household away from a mining area consumes."

I do some quick mental calculations using an average weight of 220 pounds for an adult sambar deer and 110 pounds for a wild boar, and figuring on at least 2,000 mining households in the val- ley. Even without considering the lower dressed weights of killed animals and the additional consumption by non-mining households throughout the valley, I figure that at least 1,000 sambar deer and

500 wild boar are being killed each year. Just from the pictures in the camera traps, it is clear that the numbers of sambar deer and wild boar right now are not extremely high to begin with. This much tiger food removed from the forest could spell disaster for a tiger population already at low densities.

While tigers can be prolific breeders when protected, critically low numbers of tigers struggling to find food may not be able to rebound. Our camera-trap photos alone cannot give some of the additional information we need in order to further assess the situation, such as prey densities and the age and sex ratios of the remaining tiger population. Female tigers have their first litter only after three to four years of age. After that, the average lifetime reproductive success for females and males is only about four and six years, respectively. And while a single female litter can average two to three cubs, there is a more than 33 percent chance that these cubs will die during their first year. So the ability of any tiger to produce numerous healthy offspring during its lifetime is limited by many factors, poaching aside.

Even if we were to stop the hunting of tigers, we also have to deal with the accelerated loss of the tiger's prey brought about by the market demand for food near the gold mines. An average tiger needs a minimum of 6,600 pounds of meat, or about fifty large ungulates a year, to survive. Just from our first rough estimates of what is happening at the gold mines, we can tell that hunters are removing enough sambar deer and wild pig alone to be feeding as many as thirty tigers in a year, more than the current number estimated to be living in the wildlife sanctuary. Prey depletion of this magnitude has to be stopped if tigers are to be saved. When prey levels drop too low, threatening the nutrition of the tiger population, a relatively small increase in poaching of an already small tiger population can trigger extinction.

We are at a critical nexus in the valley and have a lot of forces working against tiger abundance right now. Tiger poaching stretching over decades is the most obvious reason for low tiger densities.

But the rapid deterioration of the prey base appears to be recent. This gives me hope that we can reverse the trend, although if current activities continue unabated, the future of this area as a tiger reserve is in grave doubt.

Part of me wants to immediately abandon the idea of protecting the whole valley so that we can circle our wagons and use all our resources on behalf of the existing wildlife sanctuary. But the stronger voice in my head says that the likely reason we have any tigers left at all here is because of the vastness and diversity of this valley. We have to try to save it all.

"We need to focus more strongly on protecting the core wildlife sanctuary, while getting more data in other parts of the valley," I say to Myint Maung after giving him my analysis of the situation as best I can. He nods his agreement.

"We also have to be more selective in picking our next areas for the camera-trap grids." I grab some maps to spread before us. "The next one should be near a gold mine. We need more information on the effects of all this hunting. There's a lot more hard work ahead."

"Three of the men are down with malaria," Myint Maung says, which means our camera-trap teams are now cut by a third.

"Do what you can," I say, knowing that these men almost kill themselves trying to get their job done.

I turn to Khin Dtay.

"Your job is more important now than ever. The information you've already given us is invaluable. But we need much more data on what and where people are hunting, what they are eating, and what they are selling. We also need to know how they feel about living with tigers and other wildlife."

Khin Dtay smiles. She loves the challenges of this work. The more I ask her to do, the more excited she gets.

Suddenly a strange face materializes beside me, holding the sheets of photos I had put aside. He is pointing at some of the pictures and talking rapidly to Myint Maung.

"That's Ah Phyu," Saw Htoo Tha Po informs me. "He's one of the best Lisu hunters in the valley. He works for us now, sort of. He's telling Myint Maung he knows the people in the pictures. They are Lisu from Putao coming in along the Taron River. But the people in green uniforms he says are KIA."

"Where are the KIA coming from?" I ask.

"From Aung Leuk, their camp on the Tanai River," Saw Htoo Tha Po says, pointing to a spot on the map in front of me.

"What?" I raise my voice without thinking. I knew they had a jungle camp inside the valley, but no one ever told me where—until now. "Their base is inside the wildlife sanctuary?"

"No, no," says Myint Maung. "We ended up drawing the final boundaries of the wildlife sanctuary around the KIA camp."

"Great," I say shaking my head. "So the KIA base sits right on the Tanai River, sticking like an appendage into the wildlife sanctuary. One more issue to deal with."

I ask Saw Tun Khaing to request permission from the KIA and from the government authorities for us to visit Aung Leuk as soon as possible. I haven't thought much about the KIA's presence in the valley until now. I am still unclear about their relationship with the government, their authority in the valley, and my ability to interact with them. But I've been told that they are one of the only insurgent groups who maintain strict hunting regulations against tigers, leopards, and elephants. Now I learn that the KIA also pays hunters to supply their gold mining camps with wild meat. Perhaps that explains the camera-trap photo. A meeting with these people is clearly necessary.

Two hours later, Saw Tun Khaing reports that government authorities won't give me permission to visit the KIA camp on such short notice. However, the KIA, learning of our interest, wants to meet with us. Since we can't go to them, they will send two representatives to visit me.

At 5:30 that afternoon, just as it is getting dark, two KIA lieutenants arrive at our bungalow and are ushered to a small table we've set up with beer, soft drinks, fried chicken, shrimp chips, and peanuts. Also there to join us in this private discussion are a military intelligence officer and a policeman, both from Tanai.

I don't need to be warned against speaking too freely. Everyone is taking notes. But the rank of the officers tells me that they have been sent to listen and report back, nothing more. So, with Saw Tun Khaing translating, I explain who I am, the history of WCS's involvement in the Hukawng, and what we are trying to do now. I know full well that the KIA, like Military Intelligence, keeps track of my activities and already knows most of what I am telling them. But I need to reassure them that there is no hidden agenda.

Unrolling a map of the valley, I point out the boundaries of the new wildlife sanctuary, making sure I exclude the KIA's base at Aung Leuk. I commend the KIA for their restrictions on killing certain species, but then I explain the functional relationship between tigers and the food they eat. If the tiger's food is wiped out, you might as well be putting a bullet into the head of the tigers themselves, I say. I decide not to mention the photographs we have of their soldiers hunting, or the latest idea by the government—to protect wildlife in the entire valley.

Strangely, I've come to love this part of my work. Meeting with an insurgent army in some bustling little backwoods town, trying to convince them against all odds that they should help us protect tigers and other wildlife. Discussing poaching, gold mining, and forest destruction for opium production, knowing full well that they are involved in all of it. Government agents watching and recording what I do and say. This is the side of conservation that few people ever hear about or experience. But this is often how progress is made.

I hand the two lieutenants a copy of *Beyond the Last Village* as a present for the KIA commander, asking them to let him know that I wish to visit with him at his field camp when I return next dry season. Then I nod to Saw Tun Khaing, indicating that I am finished talking, before stepping away from the table. It is important to leave them alone now so that they can comfortably eat, drink, and talk among themselves in Burmese. I will learn later from Saw Tun Khaing what they talk about without me there.

﹏

AT MY REQUEST, Ah Phyu doesn't go into the field with the camera-trap team the next day. Instead, he takes me to his home village of Lamon, a Lisu settlement renowned for its hunters. On the way we stop at another Lisu village, called Taron, where a hunter he knows has just killed a bear and a gaur. The hunter recounts his exploits freely, showing me the bear skin and explaining that the gall bladder has already been sent to Myitkyina for sale; he had roasted and eaten the bear paws the previous night. I spot the gaur head drying out over his fireplace.

Until I learned of the KIA's involvement in hunting, the Lisu were my greatest concern. Many came into the valley with the gold mining boom. With their epicenter in Putao, it is the Lisu who continually move about, venturing deep into the forest after gaur, tigers, river otters, or elephants, then selling the valued body parts to traders from China. Steel-jaw traps and metal snares are often their weapons of choice. During my years of exploration in northern Myanmar, it was the Lisu, often far from home, whom I'd continually encounter deep in the wilderness.

When we arrive in Lamon, Ah Phyu directs me to a little thatched stand alongside the road. A woman beckons us in. This is Ah Phyu's own little stop-and-shop that he recently built for passing vehicles wanting tea, powdered coffee mix, peanuts, or some candies.

"The Naga are fierce," Ah Phyu says when I tell him of my time with them in the mountains during my last trip in 1999. We are relaxing in his shop, sipping coffee and watching the trucks kick up clouds of dust as they pass.

"But they go where no one else wants to be. They like to hunt with spears, but now they have guns. Lisu hunt all over. We like the forest. If we hear about animals somewhere—we go. Some Lisu still use crossbows, but now many also have guns. In the Hukawng there are still many animals around. And now there is also gold."

"Do the Lisu dig for gold?" I ask.

"Sometimes, but many Lisu get money by hunting and selling the meat in the camps. Now some start shops like mine," he says proudly.

"Now you also work for us," I say.

"Sometimes." He smiles. Myint Maung complains that Ah Phyu simply packs up and disappears when something elsewhere strikes his fancy.

"Can we stop the Lisu from killing tiger and other animals in here? Will you help us do that?" I ask.

"If Lisu can kill a tiger, they will kill it," he replies honestly. "There is not much I can do. They make good money from the *law pan* [traders]."

He stands and walks to his hut a short distance away. I follow.

Inside the hut, Ah Phyu stokes the coals in the hearth to boil water for tea. As the fire comes to life, the light from the flames illuminates an extensive collection of animal skulls attached to a bamboo frame on one of the walls. I've seen this kind of trophy board many times before during our hikes up north. The Lisu believe that if they save and respect the skulls of their kills, they will have better luck in hunting that same species in the future. The idea is not far removed from the Naga belief that you consume a killed animal's life force when you eat it.

"What does everyone do back here during the rainy season?" I ask.

"Before last year, not so many people came in here, especially during the rains. Travel is hard. Many people get sick and die. Now, with the road, it is better," he says.

"Is everything better for you now?" Ah Phyu is quiet for a moment.

"There are too many strangers back here. Many are not good. The animals are dying too fast." He glances at the trophy board.

"How much longer will you hunt, Ah Phyu?" I ask.

"Maybe it is time to stop," he says thoughtfully.

"Maybe I will help you."

❧ CHAPTER 10 ❧

Conservation Warfare

AFTER MY 2002 TRIP into the Hukawng Valley, I know I am racing the clock. Though I had tried to imagine what changes would take place in the months ahead when first speaking with the minister of forestry, I never anticipated the sudden fixing of the bridges, the rapid influx of humans, the presence of organized gold mining, the increased levels of wildlife poaching for commercial sale of meat and animal parts, or the involvement of the KIA. I had asked for a three-year grace period before formalizing the protection of the entire tiger reserve so that we would have sufficient data to inform us about how, or even whether, to move forward. It was wishful thinking.

Back in my study in New York, I repeatedly replay in my mind the last conversation I had with Ah Phyu. One of the best Lisu hunters in the Hukawng had all but told me he was going to give up hunting. Something about killing seemed distasteful to him since the gold mines had opened up the valley. I couldn't figure out what had triggered such a change in the heart and mind of a Lisu who had always lived by a certain set of rules. Eventually I stopped puzzling over it. Other Lisu still hunt tigers in the Hukawng, and many others are now killing wildlife for profit. It was money, not morals, that was driving most hunters' actions.

Over and over again, hunters tell me that the killing of tigers in the Hukawng Valley is a practice that has been going on for decades. The stories always end the same, with the bones and skin, and perhaps the teeth, sold to a local trader or carried across the border into China. No one remembers a time when there was not a market for tiger parts.

I go to the shelves and take down the most perused book in my library—*Animal Drugs* by Chinese scholar Bernard Read. First published in the *Peking Natural History Bulletin* in 1931, this book is part of a series of Chinese medical texts that documents the traditional uses of different parts from more than eighty Asian mammal species, including humans. Taken from the *Pen Tsao Kang Mu (The Great Herbal)*, compiled during the Ming Dynasty (AD 1368–1644) by Li Shih Chen, some of the remedies date back nearly 4,000 years. I turn to the section on tigers and read the first entry:

> **Tiger bones**. The yellow ones from the males are best. . . . The bones should be broken open and the marrow removed . . . acrid, slightly warming, nonpoisonous. . . . For removing all kinds of evil influences and calming fright. For curing bad ulcers and rat-bite sores. For rheumatic pain in the joints and muscles, and muscle cramps. For abdominal pain, typhoid fever, malaria, and hydrophobia. Placed on the roof it can keep devils away and so cures nightmare. A bath in tiger bone broth is good for rheumatic swellings of the bones and joints. The shin bones are excellent for treating painful swollen feet. It is applied with vinegar to the knees. Newborn children should be bathed in it to prevent infection, convulsions, devil possession, scabies and boils. It strengthens the bones, cures chronic dysentery, prolapse of the anus, and is taken to dislodge bones which have become stuck

in the gullet. The powdered bone is applied to burns and to eruptions under the toe nail.

I continue reading, amazed at the cornucopia of maladies and situations that are considered treatable by a piece of the tiger's anatomy. Everything from dog bites, baldness, dysentery, convulsions, epilepsy, sores on the penis, crying children, malaria, toothache, alcoholism, evil demons, tetanus, boils, fevers, and labor induction can be taken care of with the tiger's flesh, fat, blood, stomach, testes, vagina, penis, brain, urine, milk, bile, eyeball, feces, nose, teeth, claws, or whiskers. But of all the parts, it is the tiger's bones—particularly the humerus bones—that are considered the most useful and powerful medicinal ingredients.

Every Lisu tiger hunter I spoke with in the Hukawng Valley knew where to sell tiger bones. What they did not know was that the payment they received was only a small fraction of what others made from their efforts. In the marketplace, the value of tiger bone depends on various factors: where the transaction is taking place, who is selling to whom, the size and condition of the bones, the type of bones, and whether the bones are intact or powdered. Whole tiger skeletons can sell for US$5,000 to $10,000, while individual tiger bones range from $100–$200 to $500–$1,500 per pound. In one instance, powdered tiger humerus bone was selling for nearly $2,000 per pound in Seoul, Korea. But a Lisu hunter from the Hukawng Valley who carries tiger bones over the border into China may get only about $7 per pound. Still, with the bones of a single tiger weighing approximately twenty-two pounds, a profit of $154 to someone like Ah Phyu could help change his life.

Chinese medical texts prescribe a daily dosage of ten to fifteen grams of powdered tiger bone to stay healthy. The math is simple. It would not take very many people consuming this amount of tiger bone a day to wipe out the entire wild tiger population within a very short time. Two of the largest seizures of illegal tiger bones in India to date totaled 1,007 pounds of bones. This alone represents the lives of approximately forty-six tigers, nearly the number of tigers that might still be alive in all of the Hukawng Valley.

Of the numerous species of large bodied cats, weighing more than 80 pounds that were thought to have evolved over the last 25 million years, only seven species have survived to the present day. But even those seven species scattered over the five continents —tigers, lions, jaguars, leopards, snow leopards, cheetahs, and pumas—are at relatively low densities struggling for their survival. Among them, the tiger's struggle is the greatest. In *Why Big Fierce Animals Are Rare* author Paul Colinvaux explains how the second law of thermodynamics dictates that large-bodied predators must be relatively scarce. However, no natural law can explain or predict the behavior wrought by humans that drives a species like the tiger to the brink of extinction.

FROM NEW YORK I CONTACT Saw Tun Khaing and ask him to explain to Khin Maung Zaw and the director-general of the Forest Department that we are running out of time to save the tiger population in the Hukawng. We don't have three years, as I'd hoped. If any tigers are left in the valley by then, their prey base will be so depleted, and the human impact so extensive, that we could lose them all. I want to circumvent the agreed-upon timetable and make a new request to the minister to have all of the Hukawng Valley designated as a tiger reserve—right now!

Two months pass and I hear nothing from Saw Tun Khaing other than to tell me that the Forest Department is nonresponsive. I push the issue harder, but the same people who had encouraged me to go after protection of the whole valley now seem strangely silent. Finally, Saw Tun Khaing relays their thinking in an e-mail.

"We must stick to the agreed-upon timetable because that is what the minister is now expecting. We will confuse everyone by changing it," Saw Tun Khaing writes, parroting the words of the director-general. "The government doesn't like it when plans are changed."

"The government changes its plans with me all the time," I reply. "And I don't care who we confuse. This is what has to be done if we want to save tigers in that valley!"

I write to the minister to ask for an appointment with him myself, but my letter, sent through Saw Tun Khaing, never gets beyond the director-general's desk. He thinks that even if I take it upon myself to ask the minister to change our plans, the Forest Department will be asked to explain my actions. I understand the fear behind their reticence to act—fear of incurring the wrath of the military rulers, fear of suddenly being transferred to a new position away from family, fear of demotion, fear of losing a pension, fear at the thought that anything can be done to them without recourse. But I still must push forward, though now I have to make sure that I am the only one held responsible if anything goes wrong.

I am disturbed by the change I detect in Saw Tun Khaing, though. He has never feared bucking the system before and, having been with me on all the trips to the Hukawng, he understands why I need to shift our timetable. But this time he does little to help me. I call Than Myint and ask what is going on.

"Saw Tun Khaing is tired," Than Myint tells me. "After all the years of setting up WCS in Myanmar, fighting with the government, and traveling with you to distant places, he wants to rest. He is old now, more than sixty-five. You do not see how difficult things can be when you are not here."

"He needs a good long break," I say.

"He wants to enter the monkhood," Than Myint responds. "He wants to retire. But he said nothing to you because he does not want to disappoint you."

I talk with Saw Tun Khaing the next day, and we work out an acceptable timetable for his departure. With Than Myint having been in place for five years now, there will be no lack of continuity. But Than Myint still lacks the contacts and cachet that allow Saw Tun Khaing easy access to many government offices. I ask Saw Tun Khaing to stay at least until we have the Hukawng Valley Tiger Reserve off the ground, two more years at most. Than Myint can start taking over the day-to-day operations of the office. Saw Tun Khaing reluctantly agrees, already seeming more distant. The fire that has always burned so bright within him has dimmed.

Meanwhile, I somehow have to get through to the highest levels of government in order to accelerate the timetable for protection of the Hukawng Valley. But for the first time in years, I am at a loss as to where to turn or to whom to turn. Then, one afternoon while transcribing my field notes from the last trip into the Hukawng, I chance upon an article I'd cut out from the government newspaper, *The New Light of Myanmar*, and taped to one of the pages in my notebook. The article describes a ceremony that took place in Yangon to commemorate the fifty-seventh anniversary of United Nations Day.

I remember being interested in the piece because, as one of the few international organizations operating officially in Myanmar, the United Nations Development Programme might be able to help me with community issues in the new tiger reserve once it got established. I was also interested to learn that while the United Nations was coming under increasing pressure from the U.S. government to support further boycotts and sanctions against Myanmar, U.N. Secretary-General Kofi Annan did not think that sanctions were the way to engage with the regime.

But now, as I glance back through the article, something completely different catches my eye. The Myanmar representative at the ceremony was none other than General Khin Nyunt, Secretary-1, Head of Military Intelligence, and one of the most feared and powerful men in the current regime. He spoke words of praise for the United Nations and its efforts to engage Myanmar in constructive, nonpolitical ways. He viewed the organization as a valid platform for Myanmar's dialogue with the international community.

It would have never occurred to me on my own, but now I realize that General Khin Nyunt is *exactly* the man I need to see if I am to save the Hukawng.

Without telling anyone, I decide to write a letter to Khin Nyunt, asking for an audience. My hope is that he already knows of my prior expeditions with the Forest Department and that the proposed the Hukawng Valley Tiger Reserve has already been discussed at a cabinet meeting. I think the chances of my letter's reaching him are good. Whether or not he will even consider seeing me, however, is another matter.

Over the course of a week, I compose and then recompose drafts of a letter to Khin Nyunt. I want it to be short and informative, while sparking his interest in meeting me, without making him feel put upon in any way. Finally, I just write the letter as if I am sitting before him.

I explain the innovative idea behind creating the huge Hukawng Valley Tiger Reserve, and how it came about. I describe the concept of landscape-level conservation: combining protected areas for forest and wildlife with national and local development activities that improve people's lives. I tell him that the Hukawng Valley is the only chance we have to save Myanmar's tigers. Then I ask if I can meet him.

⚡

I HAND MY DISTINCTIVE BLUE AND WHITE Memorial Sloan-Kettering Cancer Center card over to the receptionist, who types my name into the computer and prints out a list of what blood tests are needed today. The routine is always the same: make obligatory small talk with the young, personable male or female receptionist, place the white test paper into the box outside the phlebotomist's office, wait to be called for blood extraction, wait to be called for the talk with the doctor, wait to be scheduled for my next appointment.

The waiting room is nearly full as I take one of the last empty seats. It's almost two years now since my first visit, and I've come through here enough times to know the routine. I don't feel quite the leper anymore, though I still seem to be one of the younger patients. A bald man sitting next to me converses with a friend or relative about a bone marrow match. How long before I have that conversation, I wonder?

Most people come here with a friend or family member. I won't allow Salisa to come with me, and she doesn't ask anymore. I don't want her to be part of this world. Outside this building, I can pretend I am normal. Inside, I am one of the patients. At least I know now that the progression of my CLL is relatively slow and, more importantly, I have none of the known related genetic defects that could have been passed to my children.

Nearly an hour later, I look over Dr. Nimer's shoulder as he pulls up the day's blood results on the computer screen. I know what to look for by now. White blood cell count is up to 24.5 K/ul (normal is 4 to 11 K/ul), neutrophils are down to 19.5 percent (normal 38 to 80 percent), lymphocytes are up to 74.7 percent (normal is 12 to 48 percent).

"White blood cells up a little, but nothing significant," Dr. Nimer comments. Sometimes I think I could just stay at home and play a tape recording of his words.

I remove some of my clothes and lie down on the examination table.

"Your lymph nodes and spleen are still normal," he says after prodding under my arms and pressing down on my spleen.

"Nothing happening yet. You're good to go." Dr. Nimer smiles. "Just be careful."

I leave Sloan-Kettering as I always do, with mixed emotions. I'm relieved that I don't have to face the numbers for another three to four months, but I also feel a touch of self-pity on having been forced once again to face my illness. I walk out determined to be a better father to my kids and let nothing stop the tiger reserve work in the Hukawng from succeeding.

A blaring car horn shakes me from my reverie. I'd ignored the red, flashing DO NOT WALK signal, and the stoplight had changed in midcrossing on Sixty-eighth Street. A yellow cabbie quick off the mark pulls up short as I cross his path. He makes a face and I almost do a Dustin Hoffman in *Midnight Cowboy*, smashing my fist down on his hood and hollering, "Hey, I'm walkin' here!"

But not today. Instead, I smile and wave apologetically. "Practice dying," Plato said to his disciples on his deathbed.

❧

As I PREPARE FOR MY NEXT TRIP to Myanmar during the winter months of 2003, I receive news that *National Geographic* magazine has approved my proposal, with photographer Steve Winter, for an article on our efforts in the Hukawng Valley. Steve had already gone with me on an earlier trip into the Hkakabo Razi region of Myanmar. When I saw that he shared the same commitment and passion toward conservation as I did, we became fast friends. The magazine agreed to schedule the publication of the article not long after our return from the trip in order to help my efforts with the reserve. Such an article, showing both the beauty and the conflicts we are dealing with in the Hukawng Valley, could help me with the government and inform an unaware public of the conservation potential in Myanmar.

While waiting for some answer or reaction from Khin Nyunt, I push forward with my plans to meet with the commander of the KIA jungle camp in the Hukawng. But Than Myint informs me that permission must first come from the northern commander, a major-general based in Myitkyina and the most senior military officer in the northern region. He suggests that I write a letter asking for an appointment, having no idea of the letter I had just mailed to Secretary-1.

Covering all my bases, I compose a polite, formal letter to the northern commander and run it by Than Myint for his approval. Whatever it takes, I have to engage the KIA in saving tigers. They are a major piece of this increasingly complex puzzle called the Hukawng Valley Tiger Reserve.

CHAPTER 11

Jungle Politics

I ARRIVE IN YANGON to an unexpected political firestorm of my own making. I still have told no one of my letter to General Khin Nyunt, not wanting to cause undue concern if nothing comes of it. But the general, I learn indirectly, did receive my letter. And perhaps I should have anticipated that my request to the head of Military Intelligence would spark a flurry of activity akin to hitting a hornets' nest with a stick.

Unbeknownst to me, soon after the general received my letter, Military Intelligence personnel started knocking on the doors of my closest colleagues in Myanmar. They visited our WCS office in Yangon, "requesting" files and background information on me, our program, and all our staff. They went to the Forest Department and asked to be briefed on all of our activities with the government. The minister of forestry demanded that the director-general of the Forest Department tell him what was going on and why there had been correspondence between Secretary-1 and me without his knowledge.

Saw Tun Khaing was told to appear at the Ministry of Forestry to explain the situation. The Forest Department was more than a little angry at me for circumventing the chain of command and conducting what they considered a back-door maneuver. Saw Tun Khaing and Than Myint could say with complete honesty that they knew nothing of the letter, but no one believed that I could have done what I did without their help. Than Myint felt I should have at least given him a heads-up.

Privately I apologize to Saw Tun Khaing for the angst I have caused everyone, but I am unrepentant about the action I took. After all, I did nothing other than inform Secretary-1 of our work in the Hukawng. I had tried going through proper channels, but had been put off repeatedly. I was determined to do whatever I could to get the Hukawng Valley Tiger Reserve designated as soon as possible. This initiative was not originally my idea, I remind my colleagues. Still, I am on thin ice with everyone.

Saw Tun Khaing explains to the director-general that no ill-intent was meant on my part. He reminds the Forest Department that we have nothing to hide and that all of our activities so far have been approved and received well by the cabinet. Perhaps with the publication of my book on our expedition to Hkakabo Razi, Secretary-1 is interested in meeting with me, Saw Tun Khaing suggests. Actually, I have heard nothing so far about even the possibility of an appointment with Secretary-1. Saw Tun Khaing tells me to go about business as usual. If it happens, I will be given almost no notice.

I spend a week meeting with Forest Department officials, reiterating everything that Saw Tun Khaing has already told them. The real cause of concern is the involvement of personnel from Military Intelligence, who are generally looked upon as about as subtle and polite as the German Gestapo, and who can inspire the same level of fear in people. The Forest Department is also concerned about our joint activities being put in the spotlight. The Chinese proverb "He who sticks his head above the crowd is the first to have it chopped off" is taken seriously under this regime. I try to allay their fears, wondering if I would do it again, having realized what I'd stirred up.

I would.

⚜

I AM USED TO THE MYANMAR AIR FLIGHT from Yangon to Myitkyina by now. I expect delays, I ignore the strange smells on the plane, and I take it in stride when the flight attendant comes around offering airsickness bags before the plane takes off. I am so preoccupied with thoughts of what lies ahead of me on this trip to the Hukawng Valley that the flight passes quickly.

In Myitkyina, Saw Tun Khaing, Than Myint, and I are driven to the Central Office Building for an appointment I've been granted with the northern commander. As the top military officer in northern Myanmar, he is often the last word on issues of importance in this region. This will be my first meeting with the man, and I have no idea what to expect. I need his help.

We are ushered into the office of Lieutenant Colonel Myint Thein, secretary of the Kachin State and assistant to the northern commander. A copy of *Beyond the Last Village* sits atop his desk. His brother-in-law in the United States sent it to him, he tells me. I take that as a good sign, though he doesn't say if he's read it or liked it.

Over tea, the secretary apologizes that the northern commander has been called away suddenly. I close my eyes in frustration as he explains that security concerns prevent him from saying where the general went or exactly when he will return, but it should be less than a week. I look over at Saw Tun Khaing, who shrugs. I need the general's permission to visit the KIA camp, and I also plan to ask his help in controlling the hunting and sale of wildlife meat for the gold mines. While the tiger reserve is not yet a reality, any mandate from the military is as good as law right now. I have no choice but to wait.

I ask Tony Lynam and Myint Maung, who are both now with the tiger team in the Hukawng, to meet me in Myitkyina. We need to reexamine the survey protocol for areas outside the wildlife sanctuary. Since we lack the time, manpower, and equipment to properly determine tiger densities over the whole valley, I want to set up two- and three-person teams that can move through areas, quickly searching for tiger sign. If I am to fast-track designation of the tiger reserve, I need some assessment of whether tigers actually exist throughout much, if not all, of the Hukawng Valley.

When Tony and the staff arrive, they brief Than Myint while I speak first with Khin Dtay. I request that her socioeconomic team start discussing the impending tiger reserve in more detail with villagers. Then I sit with Tony and Myint Maung to review their work plan. Another two men are down with malaria, so they are short-handed again. Everyone on the team now has had malaria at least once, despite the anti-malarial drugs we give them. Some of our team have almost died from continuing in the field despite their illness. Now there are strict instructions that anyone sick must come out of the field and seek medical attention immediately. The Hukawng has claimed too many lives already.

I get permission from the secretary of the Kachin State to meet with Captain K Seng Naw, liaison officer of the KIO, the administrative and political wing of the Kachin Army, with headquarters in Myitkyina. After Saw Tun Khaing introduces me and explains our mission, I listen to another speech about how much the KIA protects wildlife, especially large mammals, peacocks, and gibbons. They've also banned dynamite fishing in their areas, I'm informed. I think of the photo we have of a man in a KIA uniform carrying a dead gibbon, or the occasions when we've met KIA men shooting fish with guns. But this is not the time for confrontation, and the fact that the Kachin brag of a conservation ethic at all is something to work with.

I explain the idea of a tiger reserve that would encompass all of the Hukawng Valley, describing a multi-use scenario in which much of the wildlife and forests are protected but zones of development exist too. The communities should benefit through educational, medical, and agricultural programs that are likely to increase their productivity, income, and personal well-being, and that are directly linked to the management of the tiger reserve. He nods politely, taking notes and telling me that he'll report my words to the Kachin Central Committee. Finally I reiterate my desire, pending permission from the northern commander, to meet with the commander of the KIA jungle camp in the Hukawng at Aung Leuk.

"It is not a problem," Captain K Seng Naw says. "I will radio ahead to the camp when we are certain of your arrival."

After three days in Myitkyina, I am chomping at the bit to get back into the Hukawng. Steve Winter has already gone ahead to start taking pictures for the *National Geographic* article. By the fifth day, I have no more books to read and I am caught up on my writing. At my most bored, I read the labels on my clothing, then count the bricks in the walls. I spend a day roaming the streets and visiting the seven shops in Myitkyina selling leather jackets made from barking deer or ghoral skins. Waiting is a sport in Myanmar, and I stink at it. Finally, on day six, the northern commander returns and sends word that he'll see me.

I stand by the window next to an impressive pair of elephant tusks as the commander enters the room with an entourage of officials. He shakes my hand warmly and motions for me to sit in the chair next to his. Tea is served.

"I hear of all the work you are doing," he says immediately. "You have been in my country a long time now. You are one of us."

"Thank you," I reply. "This is what I love to do. And I have a hard time staying away from Myanmar for long when there is so much for me to do here. Places like the Hukawng Valley are very special."

"I hear you will be meeting with General Khin Nyunt when you return to Yangon."

I hide my shock. He knows more than I or any of our staff do.

"Yes, we have some things to discuss," I say, as nonchalantly as possible.

"How can I be of help to you, then?" he asks, wasting no more time on trivialities.

"I need the help of the KIA to protect the Hukawng," I reply. "It is important that I visit their camp at Aung Leuk to speak with them. I would like your permission for the trip."

The commander turns and speaks with the secretary, Lieutenant Colonel Myint Thein.

"Your trip to the Hukawng is already approved by the Ministry of Defense," he says. "You can go anywhere you want in the Hukawng. What else do you need?"

"Thank you," I say. "We have a problem in the Hukawng right now, a big problem if we are to save tigers. The four or five large gold mining areas in the valley are destroying the land, poisoning the rivers, and killing the animals. And not even much gold is coming out of them."

The northern commander sits up a little straighter.

"My biggest problem, though, is the excessive killing of wildlife to feed the people at these gold mines. And now even more hunters are coming in just to kill certain animals, like tigers, for their parts and sell them to the Chinese. Everyone has guns in the valley. Commander, I cannot keep tigers alive if all this continues."

"People must be able to use the land," he says. His voice is sterner now. "It is for everyone. And I cannot always control how the people act. But I will do what I can. Is there anything else?" He smiles, while giving me the brush-off.

I feel I've made a mistake by bringing up the gold mines instead of just asking for his help with the guns and poaching. But I hate those mines. I can't let it go yet.

"Commander, the water is being poisoned from the gold mines," I say. "Although the land they destroy is still only a small part of the whole valley, mercury and arsenic are getting into the streams and rivers, and flowing into the Ayeyarwady. The fish that

you are eating in Myitkyina and perhaps the water you are drink-
ing is being poisoned by runoff from these mines. People's health is
at risk, and the land in those areas won't be good for crops or much
else when the mines are exhausted."

"I will look into it," he says with finality. The meeting is over.

Saw Tun Khaing and Than Myint both look at me, waiting for
me to stand and end the meeting. I stay seated.

The northern commander remains silent and looks away. I have
overstayed my welcome.

THE FOUR-HOUR BOAT RIDE to the KIA headquarters along the Tanai
River is through a part of the valley I've never seen. The river is the
boundary we delineated for the wildlife sanctuary in 1999. Now it
is in the heart of the proposed tiger reserve. During the first hour,
all I pass are cleared or degraded areas for slash-and-burn plantations. The boat continually maneuvers around fishing nets staggered
in such a way that relatively few fish make it downstream. Several
bamboo rafts and small dugouts float by us, stacked high with rattan harvested somewhere upriver and now on their way to Tanai.

The extent of human impact I see in an area I thought was still
mostly wild is getting me down when, suddenly, all sign of human
activity drops away. When I ask about the abrupt change, the boat-
man tells us that we have crossed some seemingly invisible line that
now puts us into the KIA-administered territory. For the next two
hours, a wall of forest greenery envelops us. Large fish swim by our
boat, and flocks of pink ducks and groups of green peafowl lounge
at the river's edge. Two great hornbills fly overhead as we round a
bend in the river. Finally, someone shouts and points. The village
lies ahead. Uniformed soldiers are waiting for us on the bank.

I climb up a mud embankment, assisted by soldiers who, up
close, are just young boys in green uniforms. To the left is a trail
leading to what appears to be a village; to the right is a small guard

house beside a gate that controls access to the military camp. We are taken to a guest house inside the military camp and left to freshen up. An hour later, I hear chairs being shuffled in the central living room area outside our rooms. The camp commander and three other senior KIA officials have arrived to talk with us.

They all look to be in their forties or fifties, intelligent faces hardened by a life of conflict. This is in stark contrast to everyone else I've seen in uniform so far, who seem like mostly young, innocent children. The uniform is almost identical to that worn by the Myanmar military except that the KIA insignia is a red patch with two crossed Kachin swords, called *dah*. Up until now, no one has seemed able or willing to explain to me the exact details of the peace agreement between the ruling government and the KIA. In the boat I found out that there are clear boundaries to the KIA fiefdom. Now I learn that the Myanmar government allows the KIA to wear uniforms or carry weapons only in the territory they administer.

I thank the commander for allowing our visit, then start to review again the history of WCS and the Forest Department's work in the Hukawng. After a few minutes I am interrupted.

"This is our land," the commander states. "We love and respect it. We know what you are doing here, and we support your conservation efforts. You saw on the boat ride here the difference between the lands around Tanai and our forests. The Kachin people have always been told not to kill important animals. The penalties are harsh. We need our resources for the future. Most of the killing is done by the Lisu."

"I know your rules on hunting," I say. "They are very good. And you are right that the Lisu do a lot of hunting in the valley. But it is not just the Lisu killing animals now. Not long ago the KIA agreed to the wildlife sanctuary we set up. It includes all the forest around your camp and along the Taron and Tawang rivers. But maybe you do not know what is happening when you are not there to see it," I say carefully.

With some hesitation, I hand over the packet of camera-trap

photos. This is the first time I've shown them to anyone outside our group. I watch their faces as the pictures are passed around. I see no reaction, no surprise. These men know exactly what is happening in their forest.

"Some of your soldiers use their weapons to kill anything they find," I continue. "And even the animals that you say should not be killed are for sale in the markets of Tanai and in the gold camps. Maybe the Kachin do not kill tigers, but hunters are killing all the sambar deer and wild boar they can find. This is the tiger's food. Soon, the tigers and everything else will be gone from your land."

One of the officers scowls, then says something to his friend in Kachin. The mood in the room is somber.

"We will help you if we can," the commander replies, handing the pictures back to me. "But it must also serve our purpose and serve the revolution. Remember that our people must eat. And we need money for the cause. Sometimes this causes conflict. Conflict is part of life."

"I understand about conflict," I say. "But I hope that you understand that once the tigers are gone, we cannot bring them back."

I explain, as I did with the KIO official in Myitkyina, the idea of expanding the wildlife sanctuary into an all-encompassing tiger reserve. I am careful in how I word this, avoiding details about new restrictions on hunting and forest use and the allocation of managed development zones. Later, when I am accused of having been duplicitous during this meeting, I realize that perhaps I should have been clearer. Instead, I stress the need for balance between people's needs and preserving the resources of their homeland.

When the meeting ends, I still have no real commitment from them. But I am not disappointed. The seed is planted. Creating the incentive for change is more difficult than words and promises alone. The KIA commander agrees to letting some of his people attend training and development programs that we will put in place as a precursor to the formal management of the reserve once it is designated. This is a first step.

For the rest of the day, I roam the military compound and the adjacent village where the families of the soldiers live, accompanied by a KIA captain in his twenties. I am not denied access anywhere I ask to go. The captain takes me to his house in the village to meet his family. There, over tea, he tells me the story of his recruitment two years earlier when the KIA came for him. He is not unhappy here, he says, playing with his little boy as we talk. But he hopes for a better life for his children.

That evening, in a bucolic and peaceful setting, our group is feted as uniformed teens serenade us with songs of love, family, and the revolution. In the melodious voice of youth, they sing of a troubled past and an uncertain future. I hear no sadness in their voices. They look to tomorrow with unbridled optimism.

While everyone else sleeps, I slip outside the guest house and wander a short way along a dirt tract leading toward the forest edge. I am finally alone, watched by no one. It is a cool, clear night, and I navigate only by the light of a half moon. For the first time during this trip to Myanmar, after the seemingly endless days of waiting and the countless meetings with officials in Yangon, Myitkyina, Tanai, and now here, I feel happy and optimistic.

The Hukawng Valley, a miasma of struggle and death for centuries, can now be a place of life, of coexistence between people and nature. I don't envision any Bambi-like scenario. There will be innumerable frustrations, setbacks, and challenges ahead. But the Hukawng Valley Tiger Reserve will be real, and it can be a pivotal conservation model for our time, I feel. In the end the tiger reserve might really succeed. And if it does, it will be in part because of the values and traditions of the people who live here. I suddenly understand the importance of my last conversation with Ah Phyu, the Lisu hunter, who told me it was time to stop hunting.

The next morning we carry our belongings to the river, where a KIA boat is waiting to take us back to Tanai. Saw Tun Khaing is disappointed with how little was accomplished, but I feel differently. While the appearance of conservation often occurs through sweeping mandates or sudden high-level decisions, lasting conservation comes through small, almost indiscernible changes in the hearts and minds of people over time. I am convinced that we have accomplished a bit of the latter. The real work lies ahead, though.

I stand by the river's edge while our belongings are loaded into the boat. In the corner of my eye, I see a little boy of about seven walking toward us, from the village to the military camp. He is dressed in a full KIA uniform. I point him out to Saw Tun Khaing, who calls him over.

"Are you a soldier already?" I ask the boy, using Saw Tun Khaing as my translator.

"I'm too young. But I'll be a soldier soon." He responds formally, looking both scared and impressed to be talking to perhaps the first foreigner he has ever met.

"Do you like to live out here in the forest?" I ask. "Aren't you afraid of the tigers?"

"I like animals. I'm not afraid of anything in the forest. My father says the forest is our home."

I tousle his hair and smile, thinking of my son. "The forest is the home for the animals too," I say, turning away. The boat has arrived.

"We can share the forest," he says to my back. "There is enough."

CHAPTER 12

Shaping a Miracle

I DRIVE THROUGH THE STREETS of Yangon in the back of an official black Audi with darkened windows. Other cars quickly give way to us. Next to me is the minister of forestry, U Aung Phone. We pull up to the heavily guarded gate of the Ministry of Defense, then pass through a second checkpoint before arriving at the main building. Several people are there to meet us, some in uniform. They reach down to help the minister out of the car. Less than a week ago, others in a different uniform were reaching down to help us up a mud embankment deep in the Hukawng jungle.

I am ushered with some ceremony into an ornate meeting room with plush, oversized teak furniture and asked to wait. Saw Tun Khaing arrives shortly afterward, having come in a separate vehicle. It's February 2003 and I am about to meet Myanmar's Secretary-1, General Kyin Nyunt, head of the country's infamous Military Intelligence network. I feel like a character in a James Bond novel.

General Kyin Nyunt enters the room with several ministers trailing behind. Dressed in military uniform, he is a short, lean man with jet black hair and glasses a bit too large for his face. He looks younger than his sixty-four years, but his Chinese ethnicity is clearly evident. Without hesitation he walks over, shakes my hand enthusiastically, and motions for everyone to sit.

As protocol demands, the forestry minister speaks first, explaining what the role of WCS has been and telling of my years working with the Forest Department. Kyin Nyunt nods knowingly. After the visits by Military Intelligence to our office and the Forest Department, I assume he is better informed about my life and work than many WCS staff back in New York. Saw Tun Khaing speaks next, discussing in great detail what WCS has been doing in Myanmar and our most recent efforts to save the country's tigers in the Hukawng Valley. Saw Tun Khaing finishes by saying that I've asked for this meeting to pay my respects to the general.

While Saw Tun Khaing is speaking, I watch the face of Secretary-1, reviewing some of the background research I did myself. After a 1983 bomb attack in Yangon by North Korean agents in which eighteen South Korean officials, including four visiting ministers, were killed, Khin Nyunt was ordered back to Yangon and appointed chief of intelligence. In 1988, after quelling a popular uprising, he was appointed Secretary-1 of the new State Law and Order Restoration Council (SLORC), later named the State Peace and Development Council (SPDC). His wife is a medical doctor and he is the father of a daughter and two sons, all grown.

Khin Nyunt finally turns to me. There is depth and intelligence in those sharp eyes.

"How are you feeling?" he asks, looking genuinely concerned.

I am thrown off guard. This is hardly the first question I expected from him.

"I am fine, and you, sir?" I reply.

"I mean your illness. Are you taking care of it?" The general is clearly well informed.

"I am seeing an excellent doctor in New York, but there is not much they can do for me right now," I answer.

"You know we have very good medicines in Myanmar. Some

people come here for treatment when doctors in other countries tell them there is no hope. I can arrange something here for you if you like."

I wonder what treatments he is talking about, since most people would rather go anywhere than Yangon General Hospital, a dilapidated Victorian-style building, built in 1911, where you have to provide your own medicines. More likely, however, he is referring to traditional Myanmar medicines like the kind Saw Tun Khaing is always pushing on me.

My mind races. I have very limited time with Khin Nyunt, and I need to get the conversation on track without appearing brusque.

"Thank you, General. I might need that help someday. I appreciate your concern. But right now I think the tigers need more help than I do."

Khin Nyunt nods. For the slightest moment I feel a strange affinity with Myanmar's "military strongman," whose life and purpose couldn't be more different from my own.

"So you are a man who cares more about tigers than himself." He half smiles, as if even smiles must be doled out carefully. "Well, what do the tigers need from me?"

I shift to the edge of my seat and lean forward as if the six other people in the room don't exist. A memory from twenty years ago flashes through my mind: I am standing before the prime minister of Belize and his cabinet with only fifteen minutes to plead my case for setting up the world's first jaguar preserve. I am scared and overwhelmed, feeling totally out of my depth. But I cut off the noises in my head and speak from the heart.

Now, too, I focus on the moment, explaining how dire the tiger situation really is in Myanmar and how the Hukawng is our last chance to save them. We have some good tiger data, I say, and we need more. But we are running out of time. Then I describe the recent developments that I hadn't anticipated: the bridges giving such easy access to the valley, the extent of the gold mining, the rampant hunting, the expansion of military activities around Tanai, and the influx of transients who take, destroy, and leave. I state the case for designating the entire valley as a tiger reserve *now*, which would allow the Forest Department to control the guns and stop all hunting for commercial purposes immediately. It would also set the stage for regulating or shutting down the gold mines and for working with the KIA and local communities on development projects. Furthermore, the general's support would also ensure that the military and township authorities would work with us to manage the reserve.

Khin Nyunt looks over to his aide, who is taking notes. The aide nods, indicating that he is getting everything I say. Then Secretary-1 speaks to the minister of foreign affairs and the minister of forestry in Burmese, before he turns back to me.

"There is still ongoing gas and oil exploration in the Hukawng Valley," he says. "How would a reserve interfere with much-needed activities for our country such as these?"

I knew that the Myanmar Oil and Gas Company had done exploratory drilling in the Hukawng, but their test wells had come up dry. The question he was asking was more generic, however.

"That's the great thing about how we will set up this tiger reserve," I say excitedly. "There will be extensive development zones for the people and the township, mostly along the Ledo Road. Development activities that the government deems essential can be carried out also. But most of the wild areas, we hope, would be protected as extensions to the wildlife sanctuary. This is a huge area, General. There is no reason why national, local, and wildlife interests cannot all be satisfied. But the key is to approve the protection of the area now so that we can start controlling the hunting to help the tigers. I can't do it without your assistance."

Khin Nyunt smiles. He understands the nature of my request. Following normal procedure has been getting me nowhere.

"Have you submitted your proposal to the minister yet?" he asks, looking over at Aung Phone.

"No, not yet," I answer.

"Well, you have been a friend to this country for many years. And you have done many good things for Myanmar, always in a transparent manner. Send the minister the proposal. We support your work. I will do what I can to help you."

This time, I look over to the general's aide to make sure he is recording everything. He nods at me and smiles. Secretary-1's words are mandates.

Khin Nyunt stands. The meeting is over. Saw Tun Khaing hands me the copy of *Beyond the Last Village* that I had signed for the general as a present. He takes it from me and then signals his aide, who hands him another copy of the book that he had brought with him to the meeting. I sign that one also.

"Now I have two," he says. Nodding his head good-bye, he leaves the room.

The minister of foreign affairs, who was also in the meeting, walks up to me afterward with a third copy of my book in hand and asks for my autograph.

"I enjoyed it immensely," he says. "You see very clearly."

IN MAY THE RAINY SEASON descends once again, cleansing and renewing the lands. Life-sustaining crops are nourished, and rivers are revitalized. But disease and illness abound in places such as the Hukawng Valley. Monks stay inside their temples, while villagers stay closer to home. Similarly, I return to the relative safety of my own home in the woods of New York. Life is a battlefield for me now, on many levels. If I am to continue returning to the Hukawng despite my illness, then I too must take greater precautions.

But while the physical environment cycles with some regularity in Myanmar, human affairs remain in a continual state of flux and unpredictability. On May 30, a day that is soon to be called Black Friday by the media, and three months after my meeting with General Khin Nyint, there is a confrontation along a quiet country road. Supposed pro-government demonstrators clash with a convoy led by opposition leader Aung San Suu Kyi and supporters of her party, the National League for Democracy, which won the last election in 1990 but was not allowed to take power. As many as 70 people reportedly die in the violence that follows, and Aung San Suu Kyi, who had been awarded the Nobel Peace Prize a decade earlier, is again placed under house arrest by the government. Accusations are made that the attack was set up.

In July, President George W. Bush, in an attempt to politically isolate the ruling military junta in Myanmar and force them from power, imposes sweeping sanctions that go far beyond those of the Clinton administration, banning all imports from Myanmar and prohibiting exports of financial services to the country. The WCS bank account we've used to send money to our projects there is frozen pending a special exemption from the Office of Foreign Assets Control of the U.S. Treasury Department. Meanwhile, our Myanmar staffers require funds to operate and, more importantly, they need their salaries to take care of their families.

Our lawyers at WCS try to fast-track a Treasury Department permit, but it is still expected to take months. Meanwhile, the lawyers remain adamant that WCS should abide by the sanctions. To do otherwise could jeopardize the institution's reputation and other U.S. government funding that we receive. Fortunately, travel by American citizens to Myanmar is still not prohibited.

After speaking with Salisa, I withdraw some money from our savings, then book a flight to Yangon. I started the Myanmar program for WCS in 1993, hired many of the staff, know all of their families, and feel a deep sense of responsibility for their well-being. How can you ask people to save animals, to make the world better in some of the most difficult places on earth, if they cannot have complete confidence that they and their families will be taken care of when things get difficult? In twenty years of working with WCS, we have never abandoned our field staff under any circumstances. I am proud of that fact. It is not going to change now.

In August 2003, one month after sanctions are declared, there is a major cabinet reshuffle. Khin Nyunt is appointed prime minister while still retaining the post of chief of Military Intelligence. Senior General Than Shwe remains chairman of the State Peace and Development Council (SPDC), commander-in-chief of Defense Services, and minister of defense. Five new ministers and six new deputy ministers are appointed. This is the fourteenth cabinet reshuffle since 1997.

The minister of forestry, Aung Phone, who replaced my friend General Chit Swe in the 1997 reshuffle, is himself replaced with Brigadier General Thein Aung, former deputy minister of energy. The deputy minister of forestry is also replaced. But unlike previous government shake-ups that have left us with great uncertainty, we know that this time our work has the support of the new prime minister and, I am told, Senior General Than Shwe himself.

Shortly after this latest government upheaval, Khin Nyunt, acting in his new role as prime minister, unveils a seven-point "road map to democracy" that includes permanent military participation in a new government. It is immediately criticized by the National League for Democracy. On the international scene, however, this olive branch to opposition parties is viewed as a potential step forward.

Since my successful meeting with Khin Nyunt, relations with the Forest Department have reached a new high. The director-general has forgiven my seeming indiscretion at circumventing conventional channels, and he is enthusiastic now about our proposal for the new tiger reserve. He is confident that all of our proposed cooperative activities will move forward smoothly. Consequently, as the year draws to a close, the Forest Department acts on another of our recommendations and establishes Hponkan Razi Wildlife Sanctuary, a 1,044-square-mile strip of snowcapped mountains and valleys along the India border, connecting Hkakabo Razi National Park and the Naga Hills bordering the Hukawng Valley. I had not expected this to happen while we were working on setting up the

Hukawng Valley Tiger Reserve, but the Forest Department, for the first time, had moved ahead on its own initiative. Now we finally had some leaf deer habitat protected.

The ruling I want the most happens almost a year after my meeting with Khin Nyunt. The minister of forestry approves the proposal I'd submitted to the Forest Department. On March 15, 2004, he signs the documents creating the 8,500-square-mile landscape called the Hukawng Valley Tiger Reserve. I receive the news by e-mail from our office in Yangon.

After so much effort and so little hoopla, the declaration nearly two years earlier than originally planned seems anticlimactic. But the reality of what we are now doing staggers me. We have just put into motion a reserve that is larger than forty-five of the world's countries, including Israel, El Salvador, and Kuwait, and nearly the same size as the state of New Jersey in the United States.

The lack of fanfare around such a momentous event is almost laughable. The government issues no press releases and holds no ceremony. Yet this simple act, virtually unnoticed on the world scene, not only sets new precedents in conservation but opens the door for pulling one of our most magnificent species on earth a step back from extinction. While the most important areas outside the existing wildlife sanctuary have yet to be pinpointed, and there is much to accomplish before the tiger population is out of danger, creating the legal framework for the tiger reserve is a giant step forward. The new home for Myanmar's tigers is more than half the size of all of India's twenty-seven tiger reserves put together.

I write a press release myself about the new reserve, and our public relations office at WCS puts it on the wire. Suddenly it gets picked up worldwide, and soon thereafter *National Geographic* runs an article by Steve Winter and me on our efforts to save the Hukawng Valley for tigers. Myanmar is back in the news. The government is pleased, but I am back on the firing line.

There is little time for anything else in my life other than the Hukawng Valley now. With the notification of the new reserve, our

Typical village in the remote Naga Hills north of Namyun.

Lisu "trophy wall" of monkey and deer skulls displayed
in a way believed to ensure future hunting success.

Gold mining camp at Shinbweyan, 2002.
This site was completely forested during my trip in 1999.

Local harvesting of rattan from deep inside the Hukawng Valley Tiger Reserve.

*S*unrise on the Tanai River at a bend where a tiger
had been spotted the previous evening.

*G*old mine pit at Shinbweyan in 2006,
deeper and wider than it had been on a previous visit.

Villager rafting downriver in Hukawng Valley
after harvesting palm leaves to be sold for thatching local houses.

Early morning marketplace in Tanai Town.

Traders from outside Hukawng Valley purchasing the paws of an illegally killed Himalayan black bear that will be sold as a delicacy or used in traditional medicines.

A stall in Myitkyina selling primate and deer skulls, wild boar tusks, and gaur horns. The merchant claimed that many of the animals came from the Hukawng Valley.

December 2004 workshop in Myitkyina that brought together all the stakeholders to discuss administration of the Hukawng Valley Tiger Reserve.

Author presenting stipend checks to the Wildlife Police Chief at their new headquarters outside Tanai. Reserve chief U Myint Maung stands to the far left and WCS Myanmar Program Director U Than Myint stands second from right.

One of the Hukawng Tiger Reserve patrol teams with wildlife police, forest department staff, and local guides.

Local guide closely examines
fresh tiger track to determine when it
was made, and to give an educated guess
as to the animal's size and sex.

Local hunter hides his own face with the freshly killed
sambar deer head he recently acquired.

Local people have long lived with and domesticated the elephants of the Hukawng Valley. But decades of capture and killing have decimated the once abundant wild populations. Now many residents of the valley wish to help conserve this important part of their heritage.

work begins in earnest. Most protected areas are designed to avoid incorporating large numbers of people or settlements. In Myanmar, when there are communities affected, the Forest Department must resolve land settlement issues of people living inside the proposed protected area before the minister signs off. But the Hukawng Valley Tiger Reserve is a new kind of protected landscape model, a vast area designed to incorporate both tiger habitat and human communities. At the time of signing, more than 100,000 people are living in six different townships whose administrative borders overlap one or another part of the valley. One of them, Tanai Township, is completely enclosed by the proposed tiger reserve.

Added to this complex scenario are the KIA-administered lands, Naga insurgents, gold-mining interests, and an increasing number of Myanmar military bases popping up along the Ledo Road. The challenges involved in reaching a balanced arrangement among land settlement issues, future development plans, and designated wildlife sanctuary sites important for tigers make this perhaps one of the most complex protected areas ever designed, which is why I had originally requested a three-year data-gathering period before any official action was taken. In addition to the time it will take to deal with land settlement issues, we also need to survey for wildlife throughout the Hukawng in order to delineate the other areas that we'll petition to be fully protected as legal extensions to the Hukawng Valley Wildlife Sanctuary.

The proposal accepted by the minister reaffirms the already approved boundaries of the 2,500-square-mile wildlife sanctuary and delineates new boundaries for four wildlife corridors, each two to four miles wide, strategically placed along the length of the Ledo Road. Whatever development happens along the road in the future, tigers will be able to cross from one side to the other through one of these corridors. Now we continue the daunting task of figuring out how to structure the rest of the valley to keep its wildlife inhabitants protected.

With the reserve a reality, it is time to get some consensus among the stakeholders in the valley and begin the process of developing a management strategy. After meeting with Than Myint and Khin Maung Zaw, we agree on holding a Hukawng Valley Tiger Reserve workshop in December 2004 in Myitkyina, pending approval by the government. Immediately we start drawing up a list of invitees from the Forest Department, the Department of Mines, the KIA, the Myanmar military, the police, the Lisu, the Naga, the Shan, township officials, the United Nations Development Programme, and business leaders with interests in the Hukawng.

Though I worry at first about holding a meeting of this kind in a country where a 1988 law still prohibits gatherings by more than five people, the forestry minister's response is enthusiastic. "Such a meeting is good," he says. "Perhaps you can speak with the KIA in a way we cannot. It is for the good of the country if we all cooperate."

Sometimes in Myanmar I wonder what planet I'm on.

In July, for the last time, Saw Tun Khaing walks out of the WCS office that he helped set up. In reality, Than Myint has taken over the tasks of running the program long ago, but Saw Tun Khaing's influence and contacts are indispensable right up until the end. At the time of his departure, our relations with the Forest Department are excellent, and there is a feeling in the government that Myanmar is making significant strides to save its tigers and other wildlife.

I wasn't in Myanmar to see Saw Tun Khaing leave, but I thought about him as I walked around my house in New York, looking at some of the artifacts we'd picked up on our travels together: a Buddha statue, a Naga spear, a Rawang crossbow, a Kachin sword, a Shan carving. I would see Saw Tun Khaing again, I knew, but he was entering a different place in his mind, and our next meeting wouldn't be the same.

I stop in front of a painting of a tiger that Saw Tun Khaing had given me right before one of my flights home. The black-striped coat tinged with orange and white looks realistic enough, but set against a pink, purple, and green background, this three-dimensional creation made from different-colored sand has a phantasmagoric quality to it. I think of the multicolored Tibetan mandala sand paintings carefully constructed by Tibetan priests only to be destroyed shortly after completion, a metaphor for the impermanence of life. What was in Saw Tun Khaing's mind when he bought this for me, I wonder.

"Do you still think we can pull this off?" he had said to me, sitting at the food stand in Shinbweyan two years ago earlier. I had not replied. "Yes," I say now, looking at the picture.

Two months later, just before I return to Myanmar, Saw Tun Khaing shaves his head and enters the monkhood.

In August 2004 the director of wildlife, Khin Maung Zaw, pushes through approval for yet another new protected area: Bumphabum Wildlife Sanctuary, 719 square miles along the eastern boundary of the Hukawng Valley, encompassing both sides of the Kumon mountain range. It is an area rich in wildlife, with signs of tiger traffic from the Hukawng Valley. Now the world's largest tiger reserve is also contiguous with three other protected areas: Bumphabum Wildlife Sanctuary, Hponkan Razi Wildlife Sanctuary, and Hkakabo Razi National Park. And on the other side of the border, in India's state of Aranachal Pradesh, both the Hukawng and Hponkan Razi parks are connected to the largest tiger reserve in India, Namdapha National Park, another 760 square miles.

I propose to the Forest Department that they formally designate the four contiguous protected areas on their side of the border as Myanmar's Northern Forest Complex, totaling nearly 12,000 square miles, larger than Belgium and nearly the size of the state of Maryland in the United States. This was the dream I had when first flying over this region: an enormous, intact landscape containing tropical rain forest with tigers, clouded leopards, and Asian elephants in the same protected complex with snowcapped Himalayan mountains harboring red panda, musk deer, and takin. And in the valleys and foothills connecting the two lives my precious leaf deer.

The prime minister asks the minister of forestry about the tiger reserve regularly. "It is all he seems to want to talk about these days,"

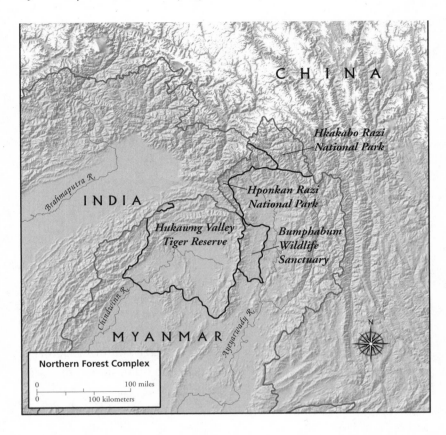

jokes the minister of forestry during one of my visits to his office. I try to keep him well informed, knowing that our reports will likely get sent to the prime minister and possibly the senior general.

PERHAPS THE CONSTANT FLOW of reports detailing exactly what we are up against in the Hukawng Valley is what does it. Suddenly there is action unlike any I would have dared hope for. The minister informs me that, upon the recommendation of the prime minister, a new wildlife police force has been created specifically for the Hukawng Valley Tiger Reserve. Since Forest Department staff have no weapons or powers to arrest people, the fifty new wildlife police will help enforce the wildlife laws. This is the first unit of its kind in the country, perhaps the region. And it shows real commitment by the government to actually help us save the tigers in the Hukawng Valley. Shortly following that announcement, the northern commander institutes a full ban on guns in the valley.

The minister asks if WCS will help fund a headquarters and housing accommodations for the police in the reserve. I agree immediately, although I realize I am putting myself and WCS in a potentially controversial position. We are already getting criticism for working with a military regime, and now I am agreeing to fund a special police force that will arrest and even jail poachers and other lawbreakers. But often the most difficult and invasive threats to conservation efforts are those that require a strong response. If I am unwilling to do what needs to be done when the opportunity arises, I should pack up and go home.

I meet with Than Myint and Myint Maung in Yangon to draw up plans and budgets for a tiger reserve headquarters, an environmental education facility, and seven guard stations along the Ledo Road. We also discuss additional stipends for the park staff and a budget for hiring more local people and daily laborers to help the staff. When I bring up the issue of the buildings and accommodations for the new wildlife police force, however, both of them fall silent.

Their reaction—profound fear and mistrust of the police in general—surprises me and dampens my euphoria. While both men understand the potential benefits of such an on-site enforcement unit, they are cynical about its chances for success, feeling that the police will take advantage of the situation in any way possible. Also, Myint Maung feels that his authority as chief of the reserve has somehow been undermined.

While I cannot change their feelings, I assure Myint Maung that he will have the final word in the reserve. This special unit was created for the Hukawng because of my constant urging to the government that we needed more help. And since it was authorized by the prime minister himself, these men are under far more pressure to perform their duties than any regular police force. This is one of the best opportunities we've been given to make the tiger reserve work, I suggest.

On October 18, 2004, while I'm back in New York, an event occurs that could be foreseen perhaps only by those closest to the inner workings of the military junta. It starts around noontime, when Prime Minister Kyin Nyunt is detained in Mandalay while on an official visit upcountry. Several hours later, the office of the chief of Military Intelligence in Yangon is raided and taken over by the army. At 8 p.m., as Khin Nyunt arrives back at the Yangon airport, he is met by General Thura Shwe Mann, the Defense Services chief of staff, and taken into custody. The official news release the next day says that sixty-five-year-old General Khin Nyunt has been "permitted to retire for health reasons."

The twenty-year reign of Asia's longest-serving intelligence chief is over. Within days, the government dissolves the National Intelligence Bureau, detains the generals who head various departments of Military Intelligence, and shuts down Military Intelligence offices nationwide. So begins the next purge of the Myanmar government. Only this time, one of the most feared and effective domestic spy networks in Southeast Asia is dismantled. Ironically, we have also just lost the most powerful ally we've ever had for the Hukawng Valley Tiger Reserve.

Though Khin Nyunt is charged with corruption, the exact reasons behind this high-level coup remain a mystery. The first theories to emerge cite disagreements over business turf, an increasingly powerful "shadow government" within Khin Nyunt's military intelligence network, and disagreements with Senior General Than Shwe and Deputy Senior-General Maung Aye. By all accounts, Khin Nyunt was the most moderate of the triumvirate, and his removal leaves a more hard-line regime in place. Soon after the incident, *The Economist* characterizes the resulting leadership as "a darker shade of bleak."

In the days and weeks following Khin Nyunt's arrest, I hear that anyone and anything associated with the general is suspect. Many government departments refuse to move on any matters, fearing their actions might be wrongly construed. The Forest Department asks WCS not to request any new trips or visas. And as for my next visit to the country, no one is sure how, or if, I will be received. Overnight I go from the status of favored son to possible pariah.

Ironically, on the heels of the purge, the October issue of Asia's *Irrawaddy* magazine publishes an article titled "The Greening of a Dictatorship." Discussing my work in Myanmar, the story suggests that I am a pawn of a government that is using conservation for the purposes of "military coercion and advancement." And as I struggle to plan our workshop with the cooperation of all concerned, the article accuses me of setting up protected areas in the Kachin State without consulting the KIA. Supposedly I am in league with the government to improve its international image, resettle ethnic minorities, and seize people's lands.

Several media outlets ask me for a response to the accusations. I accept an interview with Voice of America and say that if I am being used by the Myanmar government, they have an odd way of going about it. The only positive press releases or articles about my conservation efforts in Myanmar have been written or instigated by me. Furthermore, it is the government that insists on incorporating the local people in any plans for new protected areas. Finally, I say, if I am not consulting with the KIA, I wonder who the impostors were that I or my staff met with more than half a dozen times, and who permitted us to work in the KIA area. If this military regime wants to take over anyone's land, they sure don't need me as an excuse to do it.

Than Myint suggests that I stay away from Myanmar for the time being, until political relations sort themselves out and we know where we stand. He is unsure right now about the permission for our workshop. Meanwhile, there is a flood of innuendo and rumors about General Khin Nyunt and his family businesses. The man who used to brag about the Hukawng Valley Tiger Reserve at cabinet meetings is now said to be complicit in prostitution, gold mining, and drugs. I have no way to gauge the truth. I can't sleep at night; I can't stop thinking that everything we have taken such pains to create could collapse now or be reversed. Edward Abbey put it well in *A Voice Crying in the Wilderness*: "The greater your dreams, the more terrible your nightmares."

For some weeks there is only silence from Than Myint in response to my constant inquiries about what is going on in Yangon and the status of our workshop. I try to contact him via a third party and learn that my e-mails are not getting through. Frustrated and fearful himself, he sends a fax to me in late October 2004:

> Dear Dr. Alan,
>
> The time has come to create new e-mail account for you, since I think e-mails with your address are being watched and scanned by the government. I think the government is now shadowing everybody who had a relation with former prime minister. I think we need to create a new e-mail address for you with someone else's name. Please let me know what you think.
>
> With regards always, Than Myint

I respond by fax to Than Myint immediately: I think it is time to return.

To everyone's surprise, I am readily given a visa and granted an immediate meeting with the minister of forestry, General Thein Aung. This is a good sign. If I were out of favor, my requests for reentry into the country and appointments with government officials would be politely put off.

The minister is more formal with me than usual when we meet. As soon as pleasantries are over, he leans forward in his chair.

"We know of your friendship with the former prime minister," he says.

It is a strange twist of words, since the minister is well aware that I had only one meeting with the man. The words belong to someone else, I think.

"You know of the unfortunate events recently. Some very bad things were happening, and they had to be stopped. But we know that the former prime minister supported your conservation activities," the minister continues.

"You have done good things for the country. I have been told to let you know that the highest levels of government will continue to support your work as always. We do not want to stop the good things, only the bad."

I realize, with some surprise, that the minister is conveying a message to me directly from, or at least with the approval of, Senior General Than Shwe. Right now no else could make such statements.

A huge weight is lifted from my shoulders. Then, just as quickly, it is dropped back down again.

"There is something else we need to deal with, though," the minister continues. "I have received a letter from KIA headquarters." He picks up a sheet of paper from the table beside him.

"The KIA says you misled them. You never told them that their land will be taken away. They say they do not support the tiger reserve."

I sit back in my chair, stunned, wondering if this is related to the *Irrawaddy* article or somehow to the removal of Khin Nyunt. I shake my head in disbelief.

"I met with the KIA twice already," I say to the minister. "The last time, in the jungle, we talked about the possibility of a reserve. I explained how it will be of benefit to them. I never said specifically the reserve was going to happen, because I wasn't sure then myself. But that's the reason for the workshop in December. We want to bring everyone together, find out the needs of all the different groups involved, and let them determine what next steps should be taken."

The minister nods his head, as if the details I am giving him are more than he cares to know.

"Don't worry about the letter," he says. "I have approved the tiger reserve, and the government supports it. Your meeting will clear everything up."

Than Myint is upbeat on the ride back to the office.

"You always pull it off," he says to me, smiling. "Everything gets straightened out when you come back to the country."

But my mood is somber. We have the continued backing of the government and the Forest Department, despite the loss of the prime minister. And the workshop will go on as planned. That is all good news. But the letter from the KIA is greatly disturbing. Given the circumstances, I understand why they might think I had been disingenuous with them. Not wanting to say too much about a reserve that might never happen, perhaps I had said too little about how such a reserve would benefit them. Now they are angry. We have to fix it.

What I didn't learn until much later was that the letter the minister had shown me had already been responded to by the northern commander. He told the Kachin that they had to accept the Hukawng Valley Tiger Reserve. Had I known this, I would have been much more worried. Trying to force acceptance of the Tiger Reserve by the central government could push the KIA even further away from us. Without the support of the KIA, the tiger reserve would fail. We had less than two months to get them to the table.

CHAPTER 13

A Question of Balance

Tara pokes her head under the book I am
reading and licks my hand. I look into the droopy eyes of this sleek,
muscular, brindle-colored boxer that Salisa brought home during
one of my prolonged absences. The kids wanted a pet, she said by
way of explanation, and she wanted a protective presence in the
house. The barb found its mark. I was traveling too much.

Salisa found Tara at a rescue center in Vermont. While we were
never told exactly what she was rescued from, she was clearly thriving on our twenty-five acres of land, with two young children to
fawn over her. I scratch behind her left ear, finding just the right
spot to make her close her eyes and push her nose further into my
crotch.

Tara and I didn't like each other at first. I was the outsider,
returning two months after she had already bonded with my family. My first night home, she urinated on my clothes. I, on the other
hand, thought her overly needy, but in time we grew on each other.
Whenever she took off running through the woods or barked at
some perceived threat in the night, I was reminded of her ancient
Greek Molossian hound ancestry. I liked the idea that her bloodline
included the impressive German Bullenbeisser, a dog that once

hunted the fierce aurochs, an extinct wild progenitor of domestic cattle.

But right now Tara looks anything but fierce. She is dying.

I slip my hand from behind her ear to the lump beneath her jaw. It is bigger than it was a few days earlier, and as I slide my hand down her chest, I can feel new lumps that were not there before. Tara was diagnosed with acute leukemia three months ago, after I noticed a slight swelling of her throat. We started her on chemotherapy, although our veterinarian said it might prolong her life only by perhaps a year. One more year would have been worth it, but the chemo is making her sick and lethargic, robbing her of her appetite and, more importantly, her spirit.

I talk with Salisa about stopping Tara's chemotherapy, and she agrees that it might be for the best. But the final decision is mine. Salisa realizes that this is not only about Tara but also about me. By all accounts, chemotherapy is an assured part of my own future. Issues about quality of life are never far from my mind.

After we stop the chemo, Tara, lumps and all, becomes her old self again—needy, ebullient, and protective of the family. We have three good months with her.

Then, one morning, I wake at 5 a.m. to the sounds of scratching and thumping in the living room. I come downstairs to find Tara lying in a pool of her urine, trying desperately to stand up. I help her stand and she licks my hand. Her eyes are full of life and love, but her body has failed her. No more, I think.

In the early morning light, I clean her up and carry her out to a grassy area where she has spent so many hours playing. I wake Salisa and tell her what is happening, then wake my son, Alex, and ask him if he wants to say good-bye to Tara.

"What's wrong, Daddy?" he asks, with the sleepy, innocent look of a five-year-old. He knows Tara is sick.

"Tara's leaving us now, son. I have to take her to the doctor, but she won't be coming home again. Do you want to go outside and say good-bye?"

"Okay," he says, taking my hand.

That night, in my little cabin that I use as an office and a gym, I spread maps of the world on the exercise mats around me. It feels good to be doing this again. This is what I always do when I am finishing a project somewhere in the world and thinking about where I might go next. But the excitement I usually feel for this is replaced with the memory of Alex laying his head on Tara's body. And despite the tai chi exercises, the chi gong breathing, and the green tea intake, my white blood counts have been steadily rising. I undoubtedly still have lots of good years ahead, but right now I just need that old feeling of control over my destiny. So this time, instead of searching for my next project site, I search for where I might like to take my last walk when the time is right.

IT'S DECEMBER 2004, a little more than a month later, and I am back in Myitkyina. As I drive through the gates onto the manicured grounds of the Town Hall, I am aware that the next few hours will help determine the success or failure of the tiger reserve that has been five years in the making. I have arrived two hours early, and I pace outside the building like an expectant father as the more than one hundred invitees to this two-day workshop on community involvement in the Hukawng start to trickle in.

My stomach is in knots. After months of planning, countless hours of meetings with Myanmar government officials, and dozens of lectures and dinners to raise money for the new tiger reserve, all I dwell on right now is the possibility of failure. The KIA still has not confirmed whether or not they will attend the workshop. They continue to believe that establishing the reserve is a mechanism to take away their land. If I am not complicit, I am at best a well-intentioned pawn. That assessment may be accurate. But as any decent chess player knows, the little, oft-ignored pawn can be the most pivotal piece in the game.

In the days leading up the workshop, Myint Maung has devoted much of his energy to meeting with the KIO authorities to convince them to attend the workshop. He has explained again, as he has heard me do repeatedly, that the tiger reserve is a way to preserve their land and their cultural heritage, not take it away from them. This workshop will allow the KIA and others who live in the Hukawng Valley to voice their concerns and help structure the guidelines and management of the reserve. No one is being asked or encouraged to leave. There would be restrictions that were not in place before, yes. But those restrictions would serve to keep the valley's resources intact. The Hukawng Valley Tiger Reserve will protect the interests of both people and wildlife. Our meeting couldn't succeed without the KIA, Myint Maung told them. And if they didn't like what they heard, they could always walk out.

Fifteen minutes before the opening speech, all rows are filled except for several seats up front that we'd reserved for the KIO. I am about to ask Than Myint to drive me to their headquarters to make one last, desperate plea, when a white Toyota truck comes through the gates and pulls up to the front door. Four men I've never met before get out and enter the hallway. I am introduced to U Zaung Hkra, the deputy chairman of the KIO, and three other officials of the KIO Central Committee. They are shown to their seats, and I take mine beside Zaung Hkra. The moderator goes to the podium and opens the meeting.

Apart from a brief speech I give as part of the opening ceremony, and a slide show about our camera-trapping efforts by Saw Dtoo Ta Pho, WCS stays in the background. Khin Maung Zaw facilitates the workshop, calling various speakers to the podium, each representing a different authority, ethnic community, or interest group in the valley. By the end of the first day, many attendees express surprise at being encouraged to speak so openly and freely at such an official forum. No one remembers a meeting like this ever taking place before.

In the longest-lasting military dictatorship in the world, where unsanctioned gatherings are illegal, where ethnic rivalries are still prominent, and where there is still organized insurgency among the Naga and Kachin, we manage to create a "happening." Representatives of the Naga, the Lisu, the Bamah, the Shan, and the Kachin sit beside military officers, local police, township and district authorities, forestry officials, and businessmen. Speeches are given by the personal assistant to the northern commander, the chief of police of the Kachin State, the director of wildlife for the Forest Department, a Naga headman, and a Lisu hunter. The importance of the area is discussed along with the needs of the people. Everyone is being constructive. Over and over again the issues of human livelihood, food security, and better lives for the children are emphasized. The KIO remain silent throughout, but listen attentively.

On the second and last day of the workshop, we split everyone into working groups according to appropriate ranks and class structure. All groups are given maps of the Hukawng Valley, easels with blank paper, and markers, and asked to address the same questions: Do you approve of the idea of the tiger reserve? If not, what should happen to the land? If so, what purpose should the reserve serve for the people who live there? Apart from the existing wildlife sanctuary and the wildlife corridors, how should the valley be zoned or divided up? What do you view as the biggest problems or issues right now in the valley? We ask each group to reach a consensus by lunchtime. In the afternoon, we will compare and discuss everyone's opinions.

I wander from group to group, staying in the shadows, understanding nothing of what is being said, but watching in amazement at the dynamics taking place. The deputy chairman of the KIO is flanked on one side by a high-ranking military officer of the Northern Command and on the other by the director of wildlife for the Forest Department. None of these men from opposing sides have ever met before today. At some point in their lives, they might have been shooting at one another. Now all of them point at the map, draw lines with markers, discuss their ideas, and then redraw the lines.

Zaung Hkra appears animated and energized. I see him nod, then smile. The other KIO officials are split among different groups, all engaging in the same way. Clearly these men approve of what they've heard and seen up until now.

No one takes the scheduled coffee break, so we start serving beverages at the tables. Then lunch is put off at the request of the participants, who ask to extend the noon deadline to 2 p.m. Than Myint is taking notes as he moves among the various groups, listening to what is being said. I ask him for the highlights. Many of the ethnic groups are not happy with the rapid and widespread destruction of the forest and wildlife resources brought about as a result of the gold mines, he tells me. But they have little say in the matter since the mining concessions are out of their control, as are the resources in their own backyard. Permits for fishing rights, tree cutting, sawmill operations, rattan collection, and gold-mining concessions throughout much of the valley are controlled by the Tanai Township authorities. Farther inside the forest, resource extraction and gold mines are controlled by the KIA. This is the first I learn of this system.

"Has anyone here talked about the exact boundaries of the KIA lands?" I ask Than Myint.

"One participant said that the 1994 truce signed with the KIA gives the central government control for a distance of about three miles on either side of the Ledo Road in the valley," he answers, "but that the KIA has control beyond that."

"No one ever told us that until now. Not the northern commander or the KIA," I say. Than Myint shrugs as if to say, Of course not.

The afternoon stretches into early evening before each group has finished presenting its responses to the questions. There is active audience participation throughout the whole session. Now everyone has something to say. A local Kachin teacher translates for me. But I need no translation to understand something else I see happening around me: that animals and conservation can do more to bring together disparate cultures, ideologies, and social classes than any political oratory, pounding of fists, or aggressive actions by individuals or between nations.

In the end there is unanimous consensus that the tiger reserve is, in principle, a good thing and could be of benefit to all. But while everyone recognizes that the rampant killing of wildlife has to be stopped immediately, other restrictions, they agree, should not be put into place until alternative economic activities and incentives are provided for local communities. The township and military authorities agree to honor the wildlife sanctuary and the wildlife corridors that have already been mapped out, and to control both the possession of guns and the commercial sale of wildlife. But the exact size and extent of development zones around the Ledo Road and elsewhere must be worked out before we push for final authorization of the wildlife sanctuary extension areas within the tiger reserve.

The KIA, for their part, agree to help the tigers by stopping or at least curtailing the hunting of sambar deer and wild pig in the area they control. Representatives of WCS, local NGOs, and the U.N. Development Programme agree to immediately implement priority activities addressing issues of health, education, and agriculture for the local people. Before the end of this dry season, WCS promises to provide the school in Tanai with books and a new generator, to send medical assistants to visit villages and dispense medicines along the Ledo Road, and to take a closer look at existing agricultural practices. The Forest Department promises more staff for patrols and land settlement teams. Some of the more controversial topics, such as the gold mines and the auctioning of resource extraction permits by township authorities, remain unresolved. These will have to wait for another day.

"It's over," Than Myint says, clearly relieved when the meeting draws to a close. "It went really well," I respond. "We have some real consensus for moving forward."

But something still nags at me. While the KIO ended up saying all the right things and being actively engaged in the discussions, I still need more convincing. I want to speak with Zaung Hkra privately to see if he sincerely believes in what we are doing and what was resolved here. There is too much at stake for uncertainty.

"Before he leaves, please catch the KIA deputy chairman," I ask of Than Myint. "Ask him if he will agree to have a private breakfast with me tomorrow morning at a place of his choosing. Tell him there are things I wish to discuss only between us."

The next morning, Than Myint and I arrive early at the prearranged site on the outskirts of Myitkyina. We are shown to a table with seating arrangements for ten people, set up along the bank of the Ayeyarwady River. Not quite the cozy little meeting I intended, but at least there will be no government officials here.

I have been trying to take the measure of Zaung Hkra since he first walked through the doors of the Town Hall. A slight, bespectacled man in his sixties, he has a soft, kind face and a gentle demeanor. But when I have watched him engage with others, I have seen strength and firmness in his voice and movements.

I have a much better feel now for the KIA and their relationship with the ruling regime. In the 1960s they controlled large areas of northern Myanmar and were considered the most formidable insurgent force in the country, but that heyday is over. And unfortunately, the idea that they control their own destiny and the land they still administer is also no longer true. But it could be true in the Hukawng Valley, if we protect the land, manage the resources, and promote the economies of the local communities. The alternative, in my mind, is watching outside interests take over and destroy the valley. This would also destroy the Kachin culture.

I want to look into the deputy chairman's eyes when he tells me what he feels about the tiger reserve. I want him to know that while I understand that there are different agendas in play here, there is no agenda on my plate other than saving and protecting one of the world's best areas left for tigers and other wildlife. I also need him to know that I will continue to try to thwart any destructive and unsustainable activities threatening the integrity of the valley, such as the gold mines. This may sometimes put us at odds with each other, but if we believe in each other's desire to save what can rightfully be claimed as the Kachin's heritage, then we can work things out. Success will be achieved through balance, not conflict.

The deputy chairman arrives with a small entourage shortly after eight o'clock. He seems a different man from the one who had shaken my hand two days earlier. Now he grasps my hand warmly in both of his, then steps back for me to see him more clearly. I smile. Atop his head is a green baseball cap I had given him at the workshop. He points to the embroidered tiger under the words "Hukawng Valley Tiger Reserve" on the front of the cap and looks me in the eyes.

"This must live," he says. His eyes twinkle.

❧ CHAPTER 14 ☙

Burning Bright

THE STAFF KICKS INTO HIGH GEAR, taking advantage of the consensus developed in the workshop. As long as much of the tiger reserve outside the wildlife sanctuary is not demarcated as either extensions to the sanctuary or development zones, we risk losing control over new lands that are occupied by expanding local communities or by outside business interests. Our first priority, though, is to curb the hunting pressures on tigers and their prey. To encourage the KIA's commitment at the workshop to stop hunting sambar deer and wild pig, we distribute 200 fast-breeding domestic piglets to their villages and hold training courses in animal husbandry. I am aware that, if successful, we are creating a potential tiger-livestock conflict for these villages in the future, but right now I believe we have to ensure that the tigers just survive.

With so much to do, I spend as much time during the 2004–2005 dry season in the Hukawng Valley as possible. Some adventurous tourists venture into the area, wanting to be the first to experience the world's largest tiger reserve. A few are not prepared for what they see, expecting an India-style protected area with clear boundaries between local people and the animals, and safari-like views of wildlife. They think the reserve is already a failure because of all the human activity along the Ledo Road. Others, however, know to navigate through the settlements and look beyond what is directly in their path. These tourists get out of their vehicles to walk, take boats, or ride elephants into the interior, and are rewarded with a wild landscape that few outsiders ever experience.

Large signs have now been posted along the Ledo Road explaining the tiger reserve, with smaller signs indicating the boundaries of the wildlife corridors. Posters depicting the wildlife of the Hukawng Valley and enumerating the hunting restrictions plaster many of the walls of restaurants and government offices. The socioeconomic team, with its slide show presentations and questionnaires, is making its way to every village within the valley. Extra Forest Department staff have been tasked with documenting township and village land settlement claims. Once these are mapped, the Forest Department can develop agreements that balance what the people want and what is best for the forest and wildlife within the reserve. All other available WCS and Forest Department staff are taking part in tiger surveys or patrols.

Myint Maung focuses most of the immediate patrolling efforts inside the 2,500-square-mile wildlife sanctuary in order to secure at least that area for tigers and their prey. The wildlife police start checking local markets for sales of wild meat, and they inspect suspicious vehicles along the Ledo Road for wildlife parts or guns. Our agreement with the military and township authorities is that, during the first year, any first offender is given only a warning and an explanation of the laws of the tiger reserve. A photo is taken, and the person signs an agreement not to take part in the illegal activity again. Except in exceptional cases, no arrests are made.

The government approves visas for several American scientists who want to help us survey the valley. A team from the New York Botanical Garden works with local people on rattan cultivation and, in the process, discovers seven new species of rattan. Several ornithologists visit the wetland areas and discover some of the most important global sites for the white-winged wood duck, the lesser fish-eagle, the green peafowl, and the black-necked stork. At one site they find what they term "the world's single most important population" of the highly endangered white-bellied heron.

Some of the most interesting discoveries come from the Hukawng Valley's once-famous amber mines, where the amber, no longer sought after for jewelry, is now highly prized by zoologists. Fossils in the amber reveal a myriad of new invertebrate species: a 100-million-year-old specimen of a previously unknown species of bee that might indicate when carnivorous wasps turned into pollinating bees; the oldest representatives of one of the least understood insect orders, Zoraptera, yielding four new species and one new genus; a blood-filled sandfly with parasites that might have infected Cretaceous dinosaurs; new species and genera of the oldest known fossil ants; and a new genus and species of an arachnid.

Oil and gas exploration teams have now left the valley, apparently finding nothing of economic interest. In Shinbweyan and other areas, many of the gold pits are played out or simply abandoned. The forestry officer whose wife showed me the little gold balls from her pit three years earlier is now US$4,000 in debt and leaving the valley to find another job. Others, in similar straits, have already gone. Some people are so deeply in debt from leasing their plots and buying equipment, however, that they have little choice but to keep going, hoping for the big strike.

The valley is a quieter place now. The 2005 population estimate is 30,000 settlers and 50,000 itinerant gold miners, far below the 150,000 gold miners estimated in 2002. I can hear birds along the road again, and even the town of Tanai has become more tolerable. The best news I hear so far is that three weeks before my initial arrival this dry season, a tiger was reported just outside of Shinbweyan. Three people saw it, and no one killed it.

Myint Maung is growing into his position as chief of the tiger reserve nicely, learning to prioritize activities, manage his staff, and play both politician and statesman with the local authorities, the military, and the local businessmen. The first reserve headquarters building, located just outside Tanai and only partially completed, was submerged during the last rainy season and is now being rebuilt on higher ground.

I urge Myint Maung to work more cooperatively with the wildlife police, whose buildings are also now under construction. Although they are helping with some important enforcement tasks, the wildlife police are having a difficult time in their newly appointed role as wildlife protectors. Some of these men are seasoned officers from as far away as Yangon. Their unit was formed to stop the intensive and uncontrolled poaching in the valley, but the importance of their role was never properly conveyed to them. Told to pack up and move into the Hukawng Valley before anything was ready for them, the first wildlife police to arrive had to clear their own building site, were given only bamboo platforms to sleep on, and found no vehicles available for their use. Consequently, some of the police feel that their new posting is actually a punishment for some perceived misconduct. And with no direction from Myint Maung, they don't know what to do or how to do it.

I speak with Than Myint about speeding up the allocation of construction funds for the wildlife police compound, and I transfer additional funds for the purchase of several motorbikes. We also purchase an inexpensive Chinese truck so that the policemen's children can get to school. Finally, I convince Than Myint to deal with the clear inequities between the stipends of the police and those of the Forest Department staff. Tony Lynam agrees to return again to Hukawng and train the wildlife police in wildlife law, patrolling methods, and data gathering techniques.

I go back and forth between Hukawng, Myitkyina, and Yangon twice during that dry season for meetings with the minister of forestry, the director-general of the Forest Department, the northern commander, the police chief of the Kachin State, and the vice chairman of the KIO. The balancing act between all the various individuals and entities that can help move the tiger reserve forward is made more difficult by the inability to predict which people will be in power from one year to the next. While the politics of this country are incredibly obdurate, the faces behind the office desks seem in a constant state of flux. Over the span of a decade I have been through two prime ministers, three forestry ministers, two northern commanders, seven director-generals of the Forest Department, and four directors of wildlife. This year I break new ground with a new northern commander, a new director-general, and a new director of wildlife.

When in Myitkyina, I arrange a meeting with my friend Zaung Hkra, deputy chairman of the KIO Central Committee—the man who wore his tiger reserve cap proudly as we sat that picturesque morning by the Ayeyarwady River. After a warm greeting, he ushers me into a large room filled with KIA officers from the Western Command of Aung Leuk and officers from other KIA brigades. After introductions are made, he says he wanted these men to hear what I had to say in person.

"We appreciate what you have already done for our people," Zaung Hkra begins, referring, I assume, to the pigs we distributed.

"I hope to do much more," I respond. "Thank you for instructing the KIA to stop all hunting in the wildlife sanctuary, and to try to restrict their hunting in other areas. That will help the tigers a lot. But I am told your gold mines are still selling sambar and wild boar meat. Since our wildlife police have no authority in your areas, we can't check on anything."

Zaung Hkra nods, then speaks in Kachin to the others in the room.

"Sometimes people don't listen," he says. "Sometimes the situation is more complicated than it seems. But I promised I would help you. I have asked these men to help you as well."

"Do you still wear the tiger cap?" I ask.

"Often." He smiles. "But many people want it."

"Good," I say. "Tell them they can have the real animal soon."

Before leaving Hukawng for the last time that season, I walk up the Ledo Road to visit some of the local communities and spend time among the villagers. Their thoughts and feelings provide me with a different kind of metric for whether or not our efforts are having an impact. Most of the people here live as they have for generations. Eking out an existence from plantation crops and backyard gardens, they no longer think the gold mines will bring prosperity or better their lives. Just the opposite. And they feel quite strongly that Tanai Township officials and the local military care only about enriching themselves on the backs of the people. The tiger reserve, at this early stage, seems like just another mandate to them. Most wonder what changes it will bring to the valley and how it will adversely affect their lives.

I am confident that our future activities will better the lives of these people and their families. We are already planning to work with other organizations or bring in experts to run local workshops in agronomy, agro-forestry, animal husbandry, and health care. We are discussing plans for the funding of a medical clinic, a student scholarship program, and a farmers' cooperative. People living in the tiger reserve will have benefits that they would not have had otherwise. And as we help to better educate the youth, the hope is that they will seek better opportunities elsewhere, retaining an appreciation of having grown up in the tiger reserve. What will be more difficult to manage or influence, however, is how township and military authorities deal with the local people and land use issues in the valley. That will be a continual challenge.

❧

I SPEND THE SUMMER MONTHS in the United States, giving lectures and helping WCS raise the funds necessary to help support the tiger reserve. But the onus of working in what the press now calls one of the world's most brutal, tyrannical dictatorships makes things difficult. In May 2005 President Bush renews the economic sanctions on the Burmese government that he put in place a year earlier, describing the country as "an extraordinary threat, permanent and unusual, to the foreign policy and national security of the United States."

That same month I pull a press release off a Web site called Indiainfo.com: "China, India to Reopen Stilwell Road via Myanmar." It reports on an Indian survey team that went to China to discuss joint efforts to reopen the border crossing at Pangsaung Pass, which would allow people and motor vehicle traffic to travel from India through the Hukawng Valley, in order to reduce the distance between the two nations. There is no mention of any agreement with the Myanmar government, which, I know, has no plans to open the border crossing anytime soon. But this is definitely a portent of things to come. I realize that there is no stopping the changes that are coming to this valley.

In June 2005, the British journal *Nature* publishes "Conservation in Myanmar: Under the Gun," an article discussing, among other things, my efforts to establish the Hukawng Valley Tiger Reserve and repeating the criticism by opposition groups that working with the regime "seems to prioritize the needs of wildlife above those of a brutally repressed population." The author adds that "conservation biologists working in the country can expect to face continued scrutiny." He neglects to mention that because of our efforts local schoolchildren now have desks to sit at, the KIA has pigs to raise for food, more people will have access to medicine rather than die of disease, and fewer tigers will probably be shot or go hungry.

An online story from a Cuban newspaper, *Juventud Rebelde*, responds, in part, as I might: "If tigers could talk, perhaps they would ask Mr. Bush what protection of the environment has to do with the political problems troubling that small and isolated nation of Southeast Asia. But the animal surely would not get a coherent answer. . . ."

That same year three bomb explosions rock the capital of Yangon, killing a reported 11 people and wounding 162. The military government blames ethnic rebels and the self-proclaimed government-in-exile called the National Coalition Government of the

Union of Burma. In turn, these groups claim that the military junta is behind the attacks as part of a campaign of "state terrorism against the people." Not long afterward, the government announces that it is moving out of Yangon to a new capital it is building outside the town of Pyinmana, 310 miles to the north. The official reason given is that Pyinmana is more centrally located and thus a better place from which to serve all the country's needs. The unofficial reason is paranoia and fear.

For the first time in over a decade of working in Myanmar, I detect a clear shift in the government's attitude toward the Western nations, particularly the United States, that continue to berate and ostracize it. Any beliefs by senior officials that attempts at reform will lead to an easing of sanctions are now completely discarded. The hard-liners in the ruling regime gain greater confidence in their anti-Western thinking as they turn for assistance now to China, Russia, and India, all hungry for a share of Myanmar's natural resources. Though I continue to be granted multi-entry visas, permission for other Americans and American organizations wishing to work in Myanmar is made more restrictive. All of this bodes poorly for the protection of Myanmar's forests and wildlife.

But so far, our effort to protect tigers and other wildlife in the Hukawng Valley from the onslaught of hunting that saw its heyday in 2002 appears to be succeeding—on the surface, at least. No wild meat is openly being sold at local markets or government-run gold mines. Guns appear scarce these days, and hunters report the poaching of tigers and other wildlife to be way down, with tiger and other animal sightings near villages on the rise. Our patrols in the sanctuary encounter fewer violations each year. And the KIA claims that their soldiers are under strict instructions to cut back on hunting.

It will take several years before our camera-trap data give us the real picture for tigers. So much more needs to be done first, much of it with the people living in the region. As the outside world

comes to the Hukawng Valley, in the form of either conservationists or developers, it is imperative that, while we are saving tigers,
the people who also call this valley home are not further disenfran-
chised and do not suffer as a result of our actions.

CHAPTER 15

Return to the Naga Hills

I WAKE AT 5 A.M. in a pool of sweat. The air con-
ditioner is humming and the room is cool. I turn my face into the
soaked pillow and bang the headboard in frustration. The night
sweats have returned. First time in four years, since the leukemia's
onset. Part of me isn't surprised. Two weeks earlier I was in Sloan-
Kettering for my quarterly checkup. I felt great, but the tests said
otherwise. My white blood cell count had doubled since the last
visit. No amount of tai chi, traditional Burmese medicine, or
monk-blessed magic balls are holding back this disease. The clock
keeps ticking, and my sense of urgency is as strong as ever.

"Nothing to worry about," Dr. Nimer had said with his usual
aplomb, "as long as you feel good. There's just the slightest swelling
in the lymph nodes under one arm. Just be a little more careful, a
little more cautious."

"Tell that to the fleas and mosquitoes that bite me," I joked. But
I wasn't laughing inside. It was October, the start of the 2005–2006
dry season. I was leaving for Myanmar in a week.

I GET OUT OF BED, open the window, and watch the sun rise over the Shwedagon Pagoda, letting the cool morning air dry the sweat from my face. I always stay at the same place in Yangon, so that the immense golden dome of this Buddhist shrine that lights the night sky is the last thing I see before sleeping and the first thing I see upon waking. I never leave this city before making at least one trip to the pagoda, allowing my visual senses to be overwhelmed while feeling the quiet strength of the masses of Burmese praying for better lives and better times.

Heading back into the Hukawng Valley a week later almost feels like coming home. Except that this home is an ever-changing landscape in a continual state of disequilibrium. The first thing I see is more development and deforestation along the road toward Tanai. Since I was last here less than a year ago, a number of new military bases and a large military complex just outside of Tanai indicate some government plan that neither I nor the Forest Department is privy to. A degraded field that served during the war as a small airstrip is now a crude eight-hole golf course with a helipad. Some of the area's natural grasslands have been converted into rubber tree and sugarcane plantations.

I am less bothered by the development itself than by what these changes signify. After decades of inertia, clearly the military is tightening its grip on the area. A few trips here by high-ranking officials with a few comments, recorded by the press, that more of the land around the Ledo Road should be used to "strengthen the agricultural pillars of the country," and suddenly there is a flurry of activity, like ants serving the queen. Issues of whether crops such as sugarcane and rubber are well suited to these seasonally flooded areas are almost irrelevant.

Almost two years now after creation of the tiger reserve, we have gotten five of the six townships with interests in the valley to sign off on the land settlement issues for the reserve. The last holdout is Tanai Township, whose officials, instructed by the Ministry of Forestry to approve the land settlement documents, are now getting contradictory marching orders from the subregional military commander based in Tanai. Not sure whom they have to please the most, they continue to procrastinate.

I look out from the door of the new Hukawng Valley Tiger Reserve headquarters, sipping a cup of coffee. A curtained-off area with a bed has been set up for me in one corner of the large, open room. The other side of the room contains tables covered in maps and an assortment of animal parts collected by the wildlife police over the past few months. I'd looked them all over carefully the day of our arrival, recording the items in my notebook:

- tusks from at least fifteen wild boar
- horns from two gaur
- horns from two serow
- antlers from four sambar deer
- half-filled sack of wild boar fat
- sack of dried wild pig meat and sambar deer meat
- skin of Burmese python
- skin of leopard cat
- skull of macaque

Representing at least twenty-six animals of seven different species, this was a small haul compared to what had been gathered up in the first year of the reserve. Through the early morning mist I see people pass on foot and bicycle, then watch two bullock carts lumber by as I listen to the singing of a woman carrying goods to the market. My reverie is broken by the sound of hammers banging nails, part of the new construction that is going on all around Tanai.

On this trip I head straight for Namyun in the Naga Hills, spending a night in Shinbweyan before continuing the final fifteen-mile, five-hour drive the next morning. Seven years earlier I had walked a week before climbing the final mountain and arriving at this little military outpost in one of the most remote sections of Nagaland. On all of my trips to the Hukawng, I haven't been back here since. And with such difficult road access and so few staff, Myint Maung doesn't even have a presence up here yet. There are no gold mines in the Naga Hills, and the region's ruggedness and a still-active Naga insurgency have kept most outsiders, other than the Myanmar military, from coming into this area. All of our efforts to date have focused on the lower valley. That has to change. Lots of tigers once roamed these mountains. I know that some still do. But the Naga were one of the least represented and least engaged groups at the Myitkyina workshop in 2004, so there's work to be done.

There is an increased military presence here also. Even so, the feeling of entering a more primitive world, unlike the rest of the valley, is still tangible. Namyun now has 220 households, almost a 50 percent increase since 1999. Most of this, I am told, is a result of people in the more remote mountain areas resettling around Namyun. With no entry permitted into Myanmar from the India side, these mountains, the infamous "Hump of World War II tales," are still among the roughest and least developed parts of the Hukawng.

We continue by car for another four miles to Yaung Ngwe, a small village of twenty-five households with more than a hundred people, situated atop a ridge along a rough dirt track that was opened only a year earlier. The temperature has dipped noticeably. I sit in the cool darkness of the headman's hut, huddled near the hearth, sipping tea. Five Naga men from the village sit around me, answering questions I pose through a translator. Several women are in the adjoining room.

The wind sweeps through the open slats of the walls. I hear the coughing and spitting of the women behind the thin bamboo partition. A few young children with dirty faces and snot dripping from their noses hide behind their fathers, staring wide-eyed at me. How familiar this all feels.

Modern-day picture books still depict Naga men as proud warriors with necklaces of bear claws or tiger teeth, holding spears and wearing conical hats adorned with wild boar tusks and hornbill feathers. And some of the Naga do still have such remnants of the past, which they bring out during special ceremonies. But the Naga I face are similar to the ones I faced in 1999, only they look more beaten down. These seem the most forgotten people of the valley, hovering on the edge of survival and facing a strange, uncertain future.

Through the door of the hut I can see the steep slopes of nearby mountains, all degraded by slash-and-burn agriculture, the main activity of the Naga. The average family, consisting of six individuals, uses two acres of land for two years, then leaves them fallow for the next eight years. All they can grow on these steep slopes is hill rice, which barely meets their nutritional needs. And in years when rats infest the fields and destroy the rice, as I had seen the last time I was here, the sickest or weakest in the family don't survive for long.

"We need to help these people more," I say to Myint Maung as our teacups are refilled by the headman. "Just as we promised everyone, their lives should be better in the tiger reserve."

"We have not been able to get as close to the Naga as we have with the Kachin and some of the Lisu," Myint Maung replies.

"What about building a guard station in these hills?" I ask. "So in addition to having a presence here to stop the hunting, we have a place from which we can start distributing some medicines and other services for the people."

"I need more staff," he counters.

To that I have no reply. Everyone is working flat out, and Myint Maung is stretched to the limit. We have to get more help. With the tiger population as low as it is right now, we can't afford to be neglecting any place in the valley for too long.

Most of these Naga claim they know nothing about the tiger reserve, and when I explain the idea behind it, they seem indifferent. They don't really understand the reason for the reserve, nor do they see how it will affect them in any positive way. In any case, the idea seems strange to them. Tigers are still present in some numbers away from the villages and plantations, they say. Why protect something that is already here?

Some of the Naga still carry guns, often black-powder muzzle loaders obtained from their brethren in India. But the spears, so much a part of their traditional hunting, are long gone. Most of the animals killed are those that come around their plantations. Wild meat is shared among the villagers first, with the rest sent to the market in Namyun. Antlers and tusks are given as presents to military officials.

After leaving Yaung Ngwe we drive back down the mountain, pass through Shinbweyan, and continue south on the Ledo Road, arriving late in the afternoon at Lamon, the Lisu village of my old friend Ah Phyu, the tiger hunter. He seems genuinely happy to see me, perhaps because he has good news to report. In an excited voice he describes seeing a female tiger with cubs a month earlier. He also reports seeing two barking deer, a sambar deer, and three wild pigs within the past week.

"Are they all still alive?" I ask. Ah Phyu laughs.

"Everyone knows of the tiger reserve," he says. "It is a good thing. And we have no more guns now anyway." He spreads his arms, as if inviting me to look around for myself. Ever since the military issued a no-gun order in the valley, I've seen no one so far, other than some Naga, testing that law openly.

"I even gave away my crossbow," says Ah Phyu, surprising me.

"Do you still fish with dynamite?" I ask.

He doesn't answer.

When I return to park headquarters, two KIA representatives are waiting to take me back to their camp at Aung Leuk. Before leaving for Namyun, I'd requested permission from local authorities to inspect the progress of our pig distribution initiative there. The KIA decide to take me via another route this time, a dirt road cut out of the jungle that none of our staff even knew existed. The truck that is waiting for me is built from parts of at least four different vehicles.

As the guest I am given the front seat, or at least what's left of it, as they close the passenger door and tie it shut with a rope. There are no windows or front windshield, and the truck's modified Willys jeep engine from World War II protrudes into the cab between the driver and me. The gas tanks are large plastic containers tied to the sides of the truck with hoses running to the engine.

I think of asking to move into the open back bed of the truck with the rest of the group, but I am suddenly tasked with holding one of the gas lines so that it stays inserted into the engine. With only a partial floorboard beneath my feet and my knee less than a foot away from the engine block, I keep my face turned to the window to avoid breathing in a lethal amount of noxious gas fumes. When we hit the first big bump, my right knee touches the engine and a searing pain shoots through my leg. After several hours of this torture, we reach the Tanai River where a boat is waiting to take us across to the camp.

Little has changed here. The camp is quieter, and the soldiers I see appear younger. We visit with numerous villagers who received pigs. People who took heed of the training we provided and built special enclosures for their pigs off the ground now had more animals than before. Those who let their pigs run freely or kept them enclosed on the muddy ground had lost most of their pigs. Afterward I meet with village officials to discuss the next phase of assistance, still focusing on health, veterinary, and education concerns. Whenever I see a child pass by, I look for the young boy who on my last visit had said, "We can share the forest." Did he feel the same way now, four years later, I wonder. I never learn the answer.

That evening, I attend a special dinner and ceremony prepared for me by the villagers. I enter a large room in someone's house that is decorated for a party and already filled with at least twenty village officials and KIA officers. Only when I sit do the others take their seats. Then the music starts, and over the next thirty minutes I am treated to a display of attractive middle-aged Kachin women dressed in traditional garb, carrying baskets filled with sticky rice in bamboo, chicken wrapped in banana leaves, steamed fish, fruit, and a host of other delectables, all of which are placed in front of me.

Before the food is touched, I am asked to stand as two of the women flank me. One motions for me to lean over as she places a red cloth bag with silver spangles over one of my shoulders. The second woman hands me a Kachin sword, called a *dah*, in a silver scabbard. The owner of the house, one of the village officials I had met with earlier, gives a short speech.

"You are an honorary Kachin now. The sword makes you a warrior, and the bag is to carry more good things to us. You can think of the Kachin as your people now."

He sits, and it is my turn to speak.

"I am touched by the honor you give me today," I say, looking around and trying to meet as many eyes as possible. "I am proud to be an honorary Kachin, and I will try to always act in a way that honors the Kachin people. I will bring good things in this bag. In turn, I ask of you to help me protect the animals that live in the Hukawng Valley and are part of Kachin culture. Let me go back to my country knowing that I can always return to find the tracks of the tiger in these forests."

Heads are nodding as several young girls wearing KIA uniforms bring in bamboo containers containing some kind of fermented rice beer. Toasts are made, and are still being made hours later when we take our leave for the night.

⚘

As we pack the truck and prepare to return to Yangon, no one in Tanai takes much notice. Since the creation of the tiger reserve, my trips to the Hukawng have been so frequent that everyone assumes I will be back again very soon, perhaps within weeks. But I'm not so sure this time. Protection of the Hukawng is on the right track now, and soon my input will no longer be necessary. Also, for the first time I've grown concerned over the toll these trips are taking on me physically. I have tried to ignore my rising white blood cell count and the almost constant fatigue in order to focus on what has to be done here. But I can only push myself so much. I say nothing to anyone of these matters, though.

As I say good-bye to Myint Maung, we go over what some of the highest priorities are now. We need to have more discussions with the subregional commander about areas that we now know should not be encroached upon with new development. Most of the land settlement issues with the Tanai Township communities have been resolved, and we should be able to declare new extensions to the wildlife sanctuary soon.

While Myint Maung and I talk, I watch a young man pedaling furiously down the road on a bicycle before turning into our Forest Department compound. He comes to a quick stop, almost falling off the bike and barely avoiding a collision with our truck.

Myint Maung waves the boy over and confers with him, then turns to me, smirking.

"He wants to talk to you."

The boy faces me, a proud, stubborn look on his face. He is Lisu and looks to be no more than sixteen years old.

"I want to work with you to save tigers," he says. "We are not all hunters."

Myint Maung, still smiling, puts a hand on the boy's shoulder.

"He is Ah Phyu's nephew," he says.

 CHAPTER 16

Spots of Time

I SIT IN A HOSPITAL in Far Rockaway, New York, watching my mother die. She has been dying for a very long time. Several small strokes in recent years have left her unable to walk or speak intelligibly. Over the last year I watched helplessly as her health deteriorated further and dementia started taking over her mind.

When I was in the country, I would visit with my parents almost every week to check on their needs. Sometimes, when I would sit with my mother, she would awaken as if from a deep sleep. Seeing my son, Alexander, her eyes would light up for a moment and then, with complete mental clarity, she would recount some episode from my own childhood that I had long forgotten. We would both smile, sometimes laugh. But the moments were always short-lived. The light in her eyes would recede; then she would start to look past me as she was pulled back to that faraway, dark place where she now resided. I wished I could go there and comfort her, as she had comforted me as a boy.

After I returned from my last trip to Myanmar, my mother's health took a turn for the worse. By the time my father finally agreed that he was unable to care for her, she was sliding inexorably downhill. From then on she was bedridden, watched over by a full-time caregiver. After her kidneys failed the first time, I expected the worst, thinking every incoming phone call was from my father or the hospital. And finally, it was.

I turn to the window, looking out toward the Atlantic Ocean, listening to my father weep by my mother's bedside, comforting her as she passes in and out of consciousness. After her kidneys failed a second time she stopped eating, slipping further away from us into her own mind. The doctor ordered a feeding tube inserted into her stomach to keep her alive.

My father was so distraught that he could barely speak. But on one matter he was firm and unwavering. He would not watch my mother slowly waste away, like some neglected object in a nursing home. Several years earlier my parents had had living wills drawn up, naming me as their medical proxy. My mother's wishes were clear: she did not want to be kept alive by artificial means.

THE LAST NURSE LEAVES, having removed the feeding tube from my mother's stomach and disconnected the saline solution from her arm. It has been a week since I first asked the hospital to stop keeping her alive. Our family doctor tried to dissuade my father, who remained adamant. His wife of more than fifty years was gone, he cried. She was not coming back. This was not the way to respect her wishes. After two appearances before a panel of the hospital's legal and administrative authorities, my request, on my mother's behalf, was finally honored. We could take her home now.

On April 15, 2006, my mother lets out a final sigh and passes away. My father calls me while I am driving toward the Bronx Zoo, and I am able to reach the house while her body is still warm. I look at my mother, a simple housewife who raised three children, now the size of a child herself curled up in a fetal position, lips locked in a grimace. My father sits beside her, holding her hand, looking as small and broken as I've ever seen him in his life. I feel nothing inside.

I look around the room where she has died. A living room that was usually off-limits to us growing up. Couches and chairs, almost never sat on, covered with an uncomfortable clear plastic. A china closet with dishes and glasses I never remember us using. A clean, empty fireplace that rarely saw a fire. A wind blows outside, rattling the windowpanes. A blue jay lands on a branch in the tree in our yard.

I will remember this scene vividly whenever I think of my mother. It will come to represent all the "could have beens" in her life. William Wordsworth called such moments "spots of time," experiences so powerful that they continue to resonate with new meanings many years after.

MY FATHER, the strongest influence in my life, is now a broken man, physically and spiritually. He can barely walk and can no longer care for himself but, stubborn to the last, he fires anyone I or my two sisters hire to help him. After several falls, when he can no longer stand on his own and must crawl to where he can pull himself up and reach a phone, my father agrees to move into an assisted living facility that my wife has found for him not far from our home.

I bury myself in my work but cancel all trips out of the country. The Hukawng Valley seems a million miles away now, though I return to it often in my thoughts. Salisa, as always, tries breaking through the wall I put up around me, but I don't let her in. I think of all the times I've argued or lectured passionately on the plight of wildlife or shed tears for dead and dying animals. Yet I can't talk to the one person who loves me unconditionally. I want to tell her about the nothingness I feel about my mother's death, the anger I feel toward my father's weakness, and the fear of going for my next blood test. But I don't. She hugs me anyway.

My father insists on putting his house up for sale immediately, the home he shared with my mother for almost forty years. He accepts an early offer, wanting to close this chapter of his life. My sisters arrange for a company to sell or dispose of everything in the house. I take my father back to collect what he would like as keepsakes. This will be our last time here before strangers start walking through the house, handling and disrupting four decades of memories.

As my father sits in his bedroom staring at the empty bed, I go elsewhere in the house, leaving him to grieve alone. The idea of a tag sale, of strangers touching, assessing, wondering if our things are worth their time and money, leaves a bad taste in my mouth. I want as few personal items left in the house as possible. I go into the bathrooms, filling a garbage bag with toothbrushes, toothpaste, rinsing cups, old boxes of Band-Aids, cotton balls, lipstick containers, half-filled bottles of Tylenol, nail polish remover, mouthwash, and aftershave.

When my father finally leaves the bedroom to go downstairs, I go to my mom's closet and look into all the dark corners for valuables that might have been overlooked or stashed away. In truth, there never were any valuables. My father worked three jobs to provide for his family and to ensure that his children could attend the colleges of their choice.

I find four little bottles of my mother's perfumes all the way in the back on a shelf in the closet. I sniff each bottle, then hold them against my face. A nearly empty bottle of Shalimar brings back memories of kisses and hugs and a trip to the rides at Coney Island.

I go through my mother's dresses, skirts, and blouses, touching and caressing each of them in an almost sensuous manner. I go through her bras and underwear, finding a single earring and pieces of a cheap, broken necklace. I feel this is the closest and most personal I have ever been with my mother. Never would I have entered these drawers or handled her things like this when she was alive. I box them all, drawing the last bits of memories from the cloth. She saved everything. One dress I remember her wearing when she came into my room to find me angry and despondent, after a particularly bad day at school with my stuttering. "You will go farther than them all," she had said to me.

I had dreaded coming back to this house again, a place of few happy memories for me even in the best of times. But now I am glad. For a few hours, amid a deep feeling of emptiness, there rose up memory upon memory long buried or forgotten. I had touched my mother again.

As Thanksgiving approaches, my wife suggests that we do something special for my father. He is not adjusting well to the assisted living facility, although—thankfully—he does realize that he cannot live on his own. A man once fully in control of his own life, a man who dominated his family and all those around him, is now in control of nothing. I visit him twice a week, but our time together in his tiny two-room apartment is spent mostly in silence. Still, he seems comforted by my presence.

The winter of 2006–2007 takes hold as the temperatures drop at my mountaintop house in New York. In the Hukawng Valley, our staff gears up for another dry season of intensive patrols and tiger surveys. Physically and emotionally drained, I've made no plans to return to Myanmar right now.

Then one night, an e-mail from Than Myint arrives. Surprisingly sparse in content, its words are simple: "We have a big problem." Attached to the note is a scanned article from the government newspaper *The New Light of Myanmar.* I skim the article, then reread it more carefully.

I go to the kitchen for a cup of coffee, thinking about what the article said and what Than Myint clearly believes is an impending crisis for the Hukawng Valley Tiger Reserve. A high-ranking general with the Ministry of Defense, working at the behest of the senior general himself, had visited the Hukawng Valley and decided to allocate two large land concessions, each 200,000 acres in size, to two wealthy Myanmar businessmen for sugarcane and tapioca production. One concession, south of Tanai, overlaps one of our designated wildlife corridors and will wipe out extensive areas of natural grassland. The second concession, north of Tanai, will destroy pristine forest, much of which is inside the Hukawng Valley Wildlife Sanctuary.

Whether the general was even aware that the valley had been designated as a tiger reserve, endorsed in part by the senior general himself, is questionable. Under this regime, when a man of his rank expresses his intent, no one contradicts or discusses the issue with him. After what the military was already attempting on smaller areas of land along the Ledo Road, this newest development was not a shock to me. The senior general, once the agriculture minister, was a champion of dams and big agricultural initiatives, whether or not they made sense.

I was less bothered by the news than Than Myint expected. Other than the gold mines, most of the land-related threats have been centered around the Ledo Road, an area of de facto development zones anyway. While extraordinarily large, these latest two concessions still comprise only 7 percent of the huge tiger reserve landscape of 8,500 square miles. The real question is why this even happened in the first place and whether it signals just the beginning of a trend of large land takeovers that will destroy the integrity of the reserve.

My immediate concern, however, is to ensure that the integrity of the wildlife corridor and the wildlife sanctuary are preserved. The tigers might not survive otherwise. My thoughts turn immediately to figuring out who I need to contact in the government.

I write an urgent letter to the minister of forestry, with a copy to the northern commander of the Kachin State. Both of these men have been involved with the tiger reserve and, I believe, will help if they can. Events may have already gotten beyond their reach, however.

Brigadier General Thein Aung   10 December 2006
Minister, Ministry of Forestry
Nay Pyi Taw, Myanmar

Dear Minister,

I will be in Yangon in early January and will make all efforts to arrange an appointment at the earliest and most convenient time for you. I look forward to seeing you again. I have been keeping abreast of recent developments in the Hukawng Valley. The sudden allocation of huge plots of land for agricultural endeavors in the gazetted Hukawng Wildlife Sanctuary, the core of the tiger reserve, concerns me greatly. I have always agreed that there need to be managed development activities alongside tiger and forest conservation efforts in the Hukawng. But the central Wildlife Sanctuary area, gazetted by the Forestry Ministry in 2001, was supposed to remain fully intact and inviolate. Now I have learned that large plots of land have been given to Jadelands Company and Yuzana for agricultural development, threatening not only the most important tiger area but other riparian and seasonally inundated habitats that are important for wildlife.

Minister, I cannot emphasize enough how terrible this development will be for the survival of tigers and other wildlife species in Myanmar. The Hukawng Valley is the country's best and last chance to save tigers and many other animals that have disappeared elsewhere. The destruction and development of the forest in the heart of the reserve is the same as removing the heart from a human body. It does not matter how much of the body is left intact. If the heart is gone, the body will die. This is the same for tigers. The tigers cannot survive if much of the lowland forest is lost. Most of their food is in the valley, and

when that is gone there will be a steady decline in tiger numbers until none are left in Myanmar.

Minister, the Hukawng Tiger Reserve, and the Hukawng
Valley, is a large area. There can be significant development
activities in many parts of the reserve, but other parts have to
be left intact if the tigers and other wildlife are to survive. I
fully realize and applaud the Myanmar government's efforts to
expand agricultural development and become more self-suffi-
cient. But Myanmar is a large, fertile country with many
potential areas for development. There are very few good
wildlife areas left in the country, and there is no place like the
Hukawng Valley. No land should be given out as concession
within the designated Wildlife Sanctuary or wildlife corridors.
Also, some key riparian and wetland areas that we have already
identified need to be preserved. I implore you, Minister, to do
whatever you can to make sure that current concession boundaries or locations are changed so that we can keep the core
Wildlife Sanctuary corridors intact.

Thank you for your time and your help, Minister.

Sincerely,
Alan Rabinowitz

Than Myint and I are in almost daily contact. How strange that
just a few weeks earlier, the Hukawng Valley seemed a million miles
away and I was sure that at least another year would pass before my
next trip. Now I am back in the thick of it again. I ask Than Myint
to start setting up appointments with government officials and to
arrange permission for me to return to the Hukawng. He informs
me that some land clearing has already started in the concessions,
but very little so far inside the wildlife sanctuary. He also tells me
that the Forest Department is greatly embarrassed by everything
that has happened because they themselves were caught unaware.

Trying to put the best face on it, I consider this the first serious test of the government's will to save tigers. I want to see how the Forest Department, the guardian of the country's forests and wildlife, handles this situation. The Hukawng Valley Tiger Reserve is like a living organism, needing to be watched over, nurtured, protected, and guided. As with anything in an early stage of development, it will have imbalances that will, if all goes well, work themselves out or become less severe over time as the organism matures. There will undoubtedly be more crises in the future, some perhaps worse than this one. If this situation can't be satisfactorily resolved, I wonder, what are the chances that the tiger reserve can survive the politics of this country?

❧ CHAPTER 17 ☙

Reaching Mount Analogue

I SIT ON A THAI AIRWAYS FLIGHT from New York to Bangkok, a 747 airbus that covers 9,000 miles in seventeen hours by flying over the North Pole. It feels good to be leaving behind all the emotional turmoil of the past year. The passenger sitting next to me immediately strikes up a conversation, letting me know it's his first trip to Asia. Normally I avoid such airplane intimacy, preferring to detach myself from the place I am leaving in order to think only about what may lie ahead.

It is not so easy this time. I visited with my father last night to say good-bye and tell him that Salisa will check on him regularly while I am gone. He had little to say, staring at a blank television screen while letting out audible sighs. I watched the clock, letting the minutes tick by while feeling the all-too-familiar cramps start up in my gut. Once I left, it would take hours for the tension to fully dissipate. After fifteen minutes, my father said there was no reason for me to stay any longer. Already feeling guilty about plotting the fastest way out of there, I said a brusque good-bye.

"Why do you get angry at me so easily?" he asked. "I am sick now."

"I'm just tired and nervous about the trip," I said, putting the best face on the lie.

On the ride back home, I suddenly feel the tears coursing down my cheeks. I *was* mad at him, I admitted to myself. I was mad because he is weak and sick and will never get better. I was mad because when I was a child he hugged me too little and lectured me too much. He taught me to depend on no one but myself, and now he is totally dependent on me. I was mad because I thought he'd always be there for me, but now I have to be there for him. I didn't want to be the father to my father. He has left me while he is still here. He has died without dying.

I turn to the young businessman sitting next to me and pick up the conversation where he left off. I talk about the beauty and excitement of Asia and my own years spent living in Thailand and Myanmar. He asks what I do and as I explain the nature of my work, I realize that the uncertainty of what lies ahead, with all of its inevitable challenges and conflicts, is familiar and comfortable territory to me.

❧

I MAKE MY WAY through the cavernous structure of the new Suvarnabhumi Airport outside Bangkok and wait in line for a taxi. Surrounded by what seems like barely controlled mayhem, I turn my thoughts to the worst-case scenarios I may face in Myanmar. After thirteen years of working in the country, my gut tells me that we'll get through this latest crisis. So often the cause of problems in this military regime is a lack of communication and cooperation between different ministries and different military officers, all wrestling for power and recognition. All in all, the politics of Myanmar are not as intractable as many on the outside suppose. Nor are they so different from what I've experienced in other countries around the world.

I knew all along that economic development interests would eventually "find" the Hukawng Valley, but I thought we'd be better prepared when it did. So far, nothing before this has threatened our conservation agenda. But now I had to take a hard line with government officials. Compromising on different kinds of development in the valley is one thing, but encroachment into the wildlife sanctuary and the wildlife corridors is unacceptable—it could spell the end for tigers. As I said in my letter to the minister, if the heart is gone, the body dies.

In truth, I don't contemplate walking away or giving up on the Hukawng Valley Tiger Reserve. If there are tigers out there, we'll continue fighting. I can always ask for more land or redesign the reserve. We can start again. And again, and again. . . . until there are no more agains. We can't turn our back on the tigers now. Around the world, we are running out of chances.

In January 2006, a published report compiling the most comprehensive data sets to date had assessed the current status of tigers in the wild and suggested what needed to be done if tigers were to survive at all. Tiger habitat had declined by 40 percent in just the last decade, it found, and wild populations now occupy only 7 percent of their historic range. Furthermore, threats to tigers were mounting rather than diminishing. As an example, the report highlighted the widespread poaching of tigers in India's well-protected reserves; at least one well-known Indian tiger reserve, Sariska, no longer contained any tigers.

Of the two strategies the report suggested for saving tigers, the first—isolated reserves separating people from wildlife—was viewed as the poorer option. The authors endorsed a second approach—the creation of tiger landscapes, in which core protected areas would be linked with habitat corridors. This approach would be successful, they argued, because tiger conservation can in fact support and enhance local economies and livelihoods. This was the same conclusion I had come to years earlier when living and working among tigers in the forests of Asia. The Hukawng Valley Tiger Reserve could be the poster child for this report. We just had to make it work.

The success of the Hukaung Valley Tiger Reserve, having come even this far, is a story that needs telling and presents a model of conservation that could be replicated elsewhere in the world. The tiger is in dire need of saving, along with other large-bodied, wide-ranging species that are endangered. But the Hukaung Valley, at its most successful, cannot save the tiger alone. Only committed action and an array of creative approaches throughout what remains of the tiger's range can bring this species back from the vortex of extinction. If we are not successful, the extinction of the tiger will be a gross admission of failure, an admission that humankind has little desire to live with or tolerate nature's other advanced life forms that require understanding and compromise from us.

I BOARD A PLANE FOR YANGON, wondering how much longer it will be before all international flights circumvent this historic, decaying city. Two months earlier all of the government ministries and their staff, as well as the Central Bank, had moved the 310 miles north to the new administrative capital. Ironically, during the Japanese occupation in World War II, this area had been the base of the resistance movement of the Burma Independence Army, led by General Aung San, father of Aung San Suu Kyi. Now it is named Nay Pyi Taw— Place of a King. Than Myint and I fly there the next morning.

As we taxi to a stop on a runway larger and better maintained than that in Yangon, a WCS car sent on ahead from Yangon two days earlier is waiting for us. Nay Pyi Taw is clearly a work in progress. We drive on four-lane highways over former rice fields with no other vehicles in sight. Each government ministry, with its own campus and buildings, is separated by a great distance from the next ministry, with nothing but overgrown fields and shrub land in between. Then we take a wrong turn, and the road ends. Cloned, box-style government housing stretches for miles into the distance.

We make our way to the designated hotel zone, which contains some of the most modern, comfortable accommodations I have seen in the country. Than Myint selects a hotel recommended by the Forest Department, and I am shown to a small villa-like house with a canopy bed, a flat-screen television, and a deck overlooking the barren wastelands of future construction. The large safe and paper shredder in one corner of the room make it clear that we are not the normal clientele.

Despite his extensive schedule of meetings, the minister of forestry, Brigadier General Thein Aung, adjusts his schedule to see me as soon as he learns that we have arrived. Already waiting with him when we get to his office are the director-generals of the Ministry of Forestry and the Forest Department. Everyone knows why I am here.

"How is your health?" the minister asks before anything else. "You look tired and pale, more than the last time we met."

The minister's intuition is sharp. His look reminds me of the gaze of Min Thein Kha, the famous Seer of Myanmar, whom I'd visited some years earlier.

"I am doing okay, thank you, Minister," I reply. "I'm feeling a bit tired these days, but I'll feel much better if we can resolve this current situation."

"Well, then." The minister sits back and smiles. "You'll feel better soon. I have good news for you."

After receiving my letter from New York, the minister had taken immediate action without any further prompting. After consulting with the northern commander, he instructed the director-general and the deputy director-general of the Forest Department to go to Myitkyina, find out more about the concessions, and meet with the Jadelands Company chairman, U Yup Zaw Hkawng, who was given the concession that would intrude into the wildlife sanctuary.

By the time I had stepped off the plane in Thailand on my way to Myanmar, all cutting inside the wildlife sanctuary had apparently been stopped. The Yuzana Corporation, furthermore, had been instructed to honor the boundaries of the wildlife corridor that ran through their southern concession. Although rescinding these concessions entirely was beyond the power of these men, the minister could at least ensure that the wildlife sanctuary and the wildlife corridors remained safe.

I am thrilled with the news. It was exactly what I had hoped might happen, only this time there was no pleading or cajoling needed on my part.

"This is my country," the minister says to me. "I care about what we will have left in the future. And if I am to be the minister of forestry, there need to be forests and animals. And there need to be tigers."

That night I have dinner with the new director of the Wildlife Conservation Division, U Tun Paw Oo. He requests funds from WCS to help rebuild a hippo enclosure at Hlawga Park, a large captive facility outside Yangon. Though I'm not exactly sure where the funds will come from or why I am even being asked to fund a hippo enclosure, I agree to his request if there is a quid pro quo. I need his help in making sure that our proposals for extensions to the wildlife sanctuary move through the Forest Department expediently. Instead of having to take a step back, we are ready to move ahead.

I fly with Than Myint to Myitkyina. The days of worrying whether I'll make it out alive after another flight on Air Myanmar are now just memories. In November 2004, just before our workshop on the new tiger reserve, Air Bagan, a private air service run by a wealthy Myanmar businessman, had its inaugural flight. With only a few Air Myanmar planes still operable, Air Bagan now flies many of the Air Myanmar routes.

After the meeting with the minister, I am eager to give the good news to our field staff. I also want to see the concession areas for myself and meet again with representatives of various groups in the region. And I want to share with Myint Maung the bottle of whiskey that I had promised him during my last trip.

Waiting for an appointment with the northern commander in Myitkyina, I pay a call to the chief of police of the Kachin State, Police Colonel San Lwin. After the 2004 workshop, he had become a staunch advocate of the wildlife police force and our efforts in the Hukawng. He is now grateful for how much we have invested in training and improving the lives of the police and their families. The now forty-three wildlife police in the Hukawng are better taken care of, better trained, and better motivated than many other police around the country.

A few hours later I am at the private residence of the vivacious northern commander, Major General Ohn Myint. "Your tiger sanctuary is safe, don't worry," are the first words out of his mouth as he walks over and embraces me. "You know I love animals and will always help you when I can."

Then the commander starts to regale me with stories of new animal sightings from his recent trips around the Kachin State. Every so often he jumps up, gives orders to various subordinates, and then runs in and out of various rooms to show me gifts people have given him: a chunk of tiger bone, a piece of rhino horn, and carved elephant ivory statuettes. Finally his men carry a live leopard cat into the room.

Before leaving town I stop by the KIO office to see Zaung Hkra, who had recently been promoted to chairman of the KIO Central Committee. Since our last meeting, his instructions to the KIA about hunting and selling wild meat in the Hukawng have had a noticeable impact, Myint Maung tells me. Unfortunately, Zaung Hkra is away, but I meet his deputy, Dr. Tu Ja, a former dentist and an impressive intellect. The KIO Central Committee, Dr. Tu Ja says, has drafted a special letter authorizing free movement for our teams throughout KIA lands so that we can better monitor tigers and their prey. As I leave the KIO office, I learn that the Jadelands Company chairman has agreed to meet me for dinner.

It takes only a few minutes of conversation that evening for me to connect with this man and realize how fortunate we are that he was the one given the northern land concession inside the Hukawng Valley. Yup Zaw Hkawng is not only ethnic Kachin with close ties to the KIO, he was born in one of the villages bordering the wildlife sanctuary. He could not be more pleased that we want to protect the jungle that he played in as a child. As he recounts childhood memories, he speaks of tigers coming into the town of Tanai in the 1970s. When I ask about his plans for the concession, he frowns.

"I am in an awkward situation here," he says. "I did not ask for this land, but I was given it to develop by the most senior people. But do not worry, there will be no more cutting inside the wildlife sanctuary, and if you show me other important areas within my concession, I will protect them also," he promises.

"This is my heritage," he continues. "What kind of man destroys his own heritage?"

The next day I reach Tanai by noon with plans to spend a week with our WCS and Forest Department staff. It is immediately obvious how far efforts in the valley have progressed since my last visit a year ago. The Forest Department staff are all working as an integrated unit, not just going through the motions of their assigned tasks. They enthusiastically describe to me the new patrolling strategies, the impacts of their village workshops and environmental awareness initiatives, and the numbers of tiger and other animal signs they are finding.

Through Than Myint's efforts in Yangon, permission was given for a cadre of WCS staff and specialists to come into the Hukawng Valley over the past year: Colin Poole from New York, Ullas Karanth from India, Tony Lynam from Thailand, Simon Hedges from Indonesia, and Rob Tizzard and Will Duckworth from Lao PDR. All of them have had a great impact in training the staff and helping them to think and act on their own.

Along with Myint Maung, I visit Chief Tin Win Tun at the

recently expanded wildlife police compound. If Myint Maung once requested that we work to dissolve this force, now he credits them with the clear drop in hunting and wildlife meat sales in the valley. The police, on their part, realize that their lives are better since they began working inside the tiger reserve, and they have begun to believe in the importance of their jobs. Joint teams of wildlife police and Forest Department staff work and live together in the seven guard stations built along the Ledo Road. A new guard station is being planned for the Naga Hills, as I had discussed with Myint Maung on our last trip there.

I sit with Myint Maung and Tin Win Tun, listening to the banter and easy exchange between them as we all eat together at the park headquarters. Myint Maung has grown into his job magnificently. Confident now of financial support from WCS, political support from his own minister, and his relationships with the myriad of players in the valley, he has taken on the full persona of chief of the tiger reserve.

While I've continued to nag the Forest Department about our staffing problems, Myint Maung has devised a plan to supplement his staff and create the next generation of young, passionate conservationists. He brings on twenty-six youth volunteers, paid about $30 a month for expenses, from the various ethnic groups in the valley: Naga, Kachin, Lisu, Bamah, and Shan. This year, the Forest Department showed their support by allocating eighteen temporary additional staff, taken from other protected areas, for patrols and tiger monitoring teams during the dry season. I also learn that the Fisheries Department has approved an office in Tanai that will help Myint Maung stop illegal activities such as the use of dynamite, nets, and electro-fishing equipment in the Hukawng's rivers.

Despite renewed optimism, what these men and women face on a daily basis is no less daunting than it ever was. With forty-three wildlife police, eighteen permanent Forest Department staff, twenty-six volunteers, and three daily laborers, they are tasked with protecting and managing a reserve larger than El Salvador or Israel.

Even with the primary focus on protecting the 2,500-square-mile wildlife sanctuary, they are dealing with an area the size of Brunei and ten times the size of Singapore.

Eight cancerous tumors called gold mines continue to plague the reserve as well. In areas I thought would be completely abandoned, some recalcitrant miners simply go deeper. In Shinbweyan I stand beside a 100-foot-deep pit at least a mile long. With no cleanup or reclamation mandated, I am surrounded by a barren landscape of little green sterile ponds.

The promise the northern commander had made a year before, that he would shut all gold mines in the valley by 2007, has not been kept. But he has helped so much in other ways. We must pick our battles according to what the tigers and wildlife need the most right now. I see virtually no guns or weapons in the valley anymore, and the wildlife police now have informants in Tanai and other major markets who tell them of any wild meat sales. All gold panning that was being done in the wildlife sanctuary itself has been stopped by Myint Maung, and all new permit applications for resource extraction inside the sanctuary have been turned down.

I make my usual rounds among the villagers, most of whom know me by now. I am heartened to hear repeatedly about sightings and signs of sambar deer, wild pig, and even tiger. The number of Lisu passing through the wildlife sanctuary from Putao, whom we first saw on our camera traps, is down from 250 people last year to only 40 this year. My old friend Ah Phyu relishes the opportunity to tell me of two new tiger sightings. "They are still alive," he says, before I have a chance to ask.

I sleep better at night now. It has been five years since I took on the challenge of creating the Hukawng Valley Tiger Reserve, after that fateful dinner with Khin Maung Zaw at which he raised the idea of making the whole valley a reserve. I knew at the time how complex and difficult the task would be. Any conservation effort, especially one of this magnitude, is at constant risk in an ever-changing, resource-hungry world. So far, despite the seemingly overwhelming obstacles, we are succeeding. But the accomplishments in the Hukawng Valley are fragile, requiring constant work and vigilance to keep us from failing.

What I couldn't have known when I started, however, was that I would soon be forced to face the fragility of my own existence, and would come to realize the parallels between the human condition and the fight for wildlife—both requiring constant attention and compromise. The struggle for conservation is, after all, a struggle of life against death. There will never be an end to such a struggle. But I do believe that our efforts in the Hukawng Valley have reached a tipping point, a critical moment when everything has come together to create something new, something with a life of its own that did not exist before.

The pride and sense of responsibility for making the Hukawng Valley Tiger Reserve a success must now pass to all the incredibly dedicated individuals who share the same vision I had after first setting foot there in 1999. The centuries of fighting and death, the pointless slaughter of so many animals, the sacrifices of so many people along the Ledo Road, may finally be drawing to a close in the Hukawng Valley. There will continue to be problems and conflicts in this complex, highly diverse landscape, of course. More forest will be lost, and some tigers will still die at the hands of man. But life is the priority now. And with people such as Ah Phyu reporting sightings of tigers instead of killing them, the tigers have a home again. We have scaled Mount Analogue. The impossible no longer exists. But then, it never did in my mind.

✒

"Look, Daddy, look," Alexander cries excitedly, taking my hand and pointing to a big male tiger that was now walking toward us. I freeze, awed again by the sight before me. The tiger slumps down by a rock, seemingly content and unbothered by our presence. It is now the summer of 2007 and the small concrete cells and bars of my childhood memories have been replaced with green, outdoor space and a partition of glass at the Bronx Zoo's new Tiger Mountain exhibit.

"They're safe now, right, Daddy?" Alexander asks, referring to this cat's wild brethren, his eyes never leaving the tiger's resting form.

"They're not safe yet, Alex," I answer. "There's a lot more work to do."

"But you'll make them safe, right?" he asks.

I look into his face, both saddened and heartened by the hope and innocence I hear in his voice.

"I'll try, Alex," I say, squeezing his hand.

Acknowledgments

Throughout my career I have worked for only one organization, the Wildlife Conservation Society (WCS), established in 1895 as the New York Zoological Society. Over a twenty-five-year period, since being brought on by my friend and mentor, Dr. George Schaller, WCS has continually given me the freedom and support to pursue exploration and conservation wherever in the world I felt it was important to do so.

For the much needed—and courageous—financial support I received for my initial years of conservation work in Myanmar, I wish to thank Nancy Abraham, Michael Cline, Jane Fraser, Edith McBean, Joyce Moss, Walter Sedgewick, and the Liz Claiborne and Art Ortenberg Foundation. As the importance of our efforts in the Hukawng Valley became better known, the project received additional funds from the United States Fish and Wildlife Service Rhino and Tiger Conservation Fund, the National Fish and Wildlife Foundation's Save the Tiger Fund, the Global Conservation Fund, and the Beneficia Foundation. At present crucial and long-term funding for the Hukawng Tiger Reserve is being provided by Panthera Foundation, the Blue Moon Foundation, and the Liz Claiborne and Art Ortenberg Foundation. I would also like to thank *National Geographic Magazine* and the *Wildlife Conservation Society Magazine* for helping me get the story of the Hukawng Valley Tiger Reserve out to the general public.

My diagnosis of leukemia in the winter of 2001 was one of the lowest points of my life. In the months and years that followed, there were special friends who wouldn't let me give up despite my best efforts to shut everyone out. Jane Alexander and Ed Sherin, godparents to my children, made contacts for me at Memorial Sloan-Kettering Cancer Center and kept a careful watch on the well-being of my family. Greg Manocherian, a friend of many years, sought out potential treatments and people he thought might be of help. Greg always made sure that I had a caring friend to speak with when I needed it most. Michael Cline, a WCS trustee and a passionate supporter of my conservation work, was also a friend, always there when I needed him without ever seeming to impose. Greg and Michael both watched over me from the shadows, as they continue to do to this day.

In 2005, Michael Cline, after carefully following my travails in Myanmar, was instrumental in pushing me to put into motion a large-scale plan for tiger conservation based on what we had been doing in Hukawng Valley. Bringing his entrepreneurial skills to the table, he pledged $5 million for tiger conservation with a promise to help raise the additional funds needed if we produced a business plan for saving tigers, complete with specific goals, benchmarks, and measurements. There would now be accountability, something virtually unheard of in the arena of international conservation. Thus was born Tigers Forever, a range-wide comprehensive strategy for ensuring the survival of the world's most endangered large cat. Our goal: to increase tiger numbers by at least 50 percent at specific sites of our choosing over the next ten years. Michael's vision, passion, and commitment, have changed the face of tiger conservation.

That same year, I met another person who has both changed my life and become a close and enduring friend, Tom Kaplan. A highly successful entrepreneur with a Ph.D in history from Oxford, our commonality was his deep and lifelong passion for saving the earth's wild cats along with a determination to fulfill that passion. In May 2006, Tom created Panthera, a non-profit organization committed to saving the earth's wild cats. He matched Michael's pledge, guaranteeing Tigers Forever at least $10 million seed money over ten years. Panthera went on to form partnerships with WCS and other international conservation organizations, now providing funds to create and implement range-wide conservation strategies for jaguars, lions, snow leopards, and cheetahs. In addition, Panthera created a young scholar fellowship program and a lifetime achievement award for wild cat conservation.

None of the work discussed in this book could have been accomplished without the dedication and passion of the many people I've worked with in Myanmar. I wish to acknowledge the continued help and dedication of the Minister of Forestry, the Director-General of the Forest Department, and the Directors of the Nature Conservation and Wildlife Division, with special thanks to U Khin Maung Zaw. Those who care about tigers owe a debt of gratitude to all those Forest Department and WCS staff and Wildlife Police who work tirelessly under very difficult situations to make the Hukawng Tiger Reserve a success. My heartfelt gratitude to one person in particular—U Myint Maung. Only a man like this, with the heart of giant, can live up to the expectations that have been put upon him. The success of the Hukawng Valley Tiger Reserve is his more than any other. Finally I thank my special friends, U Saw Tun Khaing and U Myint Maung. The success of the WCS Myanmar Program, and all we have accomplished, is due primarily to the hard work, long hours, and unwavering passion of these two men. It is one thing to be dedicated when your belly is full, your family well taken care of, and the future looks bright. But to care about protecting wildlife in the very uncertain world of Myanmar today is quite another matter.

Apart from my good fortune of having Island Press as my publisher again, I consider myself very fortunate to be working again with my former editor, Jonathan Cobb. This is a far better book because of the efforts of Jonathan. I also wish to express thanks to *National Geographic* photographer, Steven Winter, who contributed many of the photos in this book. Besides being an avid conserva-tionist, Steve has become a good friend and a great partner in the field. Having had so few friends early in my life, I consider myself incredibly lucky to have now found people like Steve, Greg, Michael, and Tom. These are friends of the heart who have made it easier for me to pursue my life's passion of saving wildlife while raising a family and facing life's challenges.

My outlook on life is very different now from what it was when I first started the adventures documented in this book. In the first chapter of this book I introduce the personality of Vinegar Joe Stil-well who, considering nothing impossible, described himself as unreasonable, impatient, sullen, mad, profane, and vulgar. I might use many of these same terms to describe myself. Fortunately, the incredible woman who is my wife, Salisa, and my two beautiful children, Alexander and Alana, have tempered many of these traits in me while putting up with the others. Salisa time and again took on the many tasks involved with raising Alex and Alana so that I could continue my work and complete this book. There was a time in my life that I believed nothing was more important than my work. These three people have changed that.

Selected Bibliography

Books and Reports

Barua, S. N. *Tribes of Indo-Burma Border.* Mittal Publications, New Delhi, 1991.

Bentham, T. *Asiatic Horns and Antlers in the Collection of the Indian Museum.* Indian Museum, Calcutta, 1908.

Berlitz, C. *Native Tongues.* Castle Books, Edison, NJ, 2005.

Bryant, R. L. *The Political Ecology of Forestry in Burma: 1824–1994.* Hurst and Co., London, 1997.

Bryja, G., et al. (13 authors). *Setting Priorities for Conservation and Recovery of Wild Tigers.* Wildlife Conservation Society, World Wildlife Fund, and Smithsonian National Zoological Park, New York and Washington, DC, 2006.

Carrapiett, W. J. S. *The Kachin Tribes of Burma.* Government Printing Office, Rangoon, 1929.

Clifford, H. *Further India.* White Lotus Co., Bangkok, first published in 1904.

Daumal, R. *Mount Analogue.* City Lights Books, San Francisco, 1960.

Ellis, R. *Tiger Bone and Rhino Horn.* Island Press, Washington, DC, 2005.

Ethell, J., and D. Downie. *Flying the Hump.* Motorbooks International, St. Paul, MN, 2002.

Evans, G. P. *Big-Game Shooting in Upper Burma.* Longmans, Green and Co., London, 1911.

Ferrier, A. J. *The Care and Management of Elephants in Burma.* Messrs. Steel Brothers and Co. Ltd., London, 1947.

Furer-Haimendorf, C. *The Naked Naga.* Methuen & Co., London, 1939.

Gale, T. *Burmese Timber Elephant.* Trade Corporation, Rangoon, 1974.

Gilhodes, A. *The Kachins: Religion and Customs.* White Lotus Press, Bangkok, first published in 1922.

Karanth, K. U. *Tiger Tales.* Penguin Books, New Delhi, 2006.

———. *A View from the Machan.* Permanent Black, New Delhi, 2006.

———. *The Way of the Tiger.* Voyageur Press, Osceloa, Wisconsin, 2006.

Karanth, K. U., and J. D. Nichols. *Monitoring Tigers and Their Prey: A Manual for Researchers, Managers, and Conservationists in Tropical Asia.* Centre for Wildlife Studies, Bangalore, India, 2002.

Keeton, C. L. *King Thebaw and the Ecological Rape of Burma. Period of 1878–1885.* Manohar Book Service, New Delhi, 1974.

Lintner, B. *The Kachin: Lords of Burma's Northern Frontier. People and Cultures of Southeast Asia.* Teak House, Bangkok, 1994.

Lowis, C. C. *The Tribes of Burma. Ethnographical Survey of India, No. 4.* Government Printing Office, Rangoon, 1919.

McPhedran, C. *White Butterflies.* Pandanus Books, Canberra, 2002.

Meacham, C. J. *How the Tiger Lost Its Stripes.* Harcourt Brace & Co., New York, 1997.

Mills, J. A., and P. Jackson. *Killed for a Cure: A Review of the Worldwide Trade in Tiger Bone.* Traffic International, Cambridge, 1994.

Morse, E. *Exodus to a Hidden Valley.* Readers Digest Press, New York, 1974.

Mosser, D. *China-Burma-India.* Time Life Books Inc., New York, 1978.

Padel, R. *Tigers in Red Weather.* Little Brown, London, 2005.

Peacock, E. H. *A Game-Book for Burma and Adjoining Territories.* H. F. & G. Witherby, England, 1933.

Peers, W. R., and D. Brelis. *Behind the Burma Road.* Avon Books, New York, 1963.

———. *Beyond the Last Village: A Journey of Discovery in Asia's Forbidden Wilderness.* Island Press/Shearwater Books, 2001.

Read, B. E. *Chinese Materia Medica: Animal Drugs.* Southern Materials Center, Taipei, 1982.

Rezendes, P. *Tracking and the Art of Seeing: How to Read Animal Tracks and Sign.* HarperCollins, New York, 1999.

Romanus, C., and R. Sunderland. *Stilwell's Mission to China.* U.S. Army Center of Military History, Washington, DC, 1987.

———. *Time Runs Out in CBI (China-Burma-India Theater).* U.S. Army Center of Military History, Washington, DC, 1987.

Schaller, G. B. *The Deer and the Tiger.* University of Chicago Press, Chicago, 1967.

Scott, J. G. *Burma: A Handbook of Practical Information.* Daniel O'Conner, London, 1906.

Seagrave, G. *Burma Surgeon.* Consolidated Book Publishers, Chicago, 1944.

————. *Burma Surgeon Returns.* W.W. Norton & Co., New York, 1946.

Seidensticker, J., S. Christie, and P. Jackson, eds. *Riding the Tiger: Tiger Conservation in Human-Dominated Landscapes.* Cambridge University Press, Cambridge, 1999.

Stirn, A., and P. Ham. *The Seven Sisters of India.* Prestel Verlag, Munich, 2000.

Tilson, R., and U. S. Seal. *Tigers of the World.* Noyes Publications, Park Ridge, NJ, 1987.

Tucker, S. *Among Insurgents.* The Radcliffe Press, London, 2000.

Turner, A. *The Big Cats and Their Fossil Relatives.* Columbia University Press, New York, 1997.

Webster, D. *The Burma Road.* Farrar, Straus & Giroux, New York, 2003.

Articles

Amato, G., M. G. Egan, and A. Rabinowitz. "A New Species of Muntjac, *Muntiacus putaoensis* (Artiodactyla: Cervidae) from Northern Myanmar." *Animal Conservation*, vol. 2, 1999, pp. 1–7.

Damania, R., R. Stringer, K. U. Karanth, and B. Stith. "The Economics of Protecting Tiger Populations: Linking Household Behaviour to Poaching and Prey Depletion." CIES Working Paper No. 0140. November, 2001.

Ehrmann, M. "Gem mining in Burma." *Gems and Gemology*, vol. 9, 1957, pp. 3–31.

Karanth, K. U., J. D. Nichols, N. S. Kumar, W. A. Link, and J. E. Hines. "Tigers and Their Prey: Predicting Carnivore Densities from Prey Abundance." *Proceedings of the National Academy of Sciences*, vol. 101, 2004, pp. 4854–4858.

Kenney, J. S., J. L. D. Smith, A. M. Starfield, and C. W. McDougal. "The Long-Term Effect of Tiger Poaching on Population Viability." *Conservation Biology,* vol. 9, 1995, pp. 1127–1133.

Kingdon-Ward, F. "The Sino-Himalayan Flora." *Proceedings of the Linnean Society,* 1927.

————. "Botany and Geography of North Burma." *Journal of the Bombay Natural History Society*, vol. 44, 1944, pp. 550–574.

————. "A Sketch of the Botany and Geography of North Burma—Part II." *Journal of the Bombay Natural History Society*, vol. 45, 1944, pp. 16–30.

————. "A Sketch of the Botany and Geography of North Burma—Part III." *Journal of the Bombay Natural History Society*, vol. 45, 1944, pp. 133–148.

Martin, E. B. "Wildlife Products for Sale in Myanmar." *Traffic Bulletin*, vol. 17, 1997, pp. 33–44.

Rabinowitz, A. "Killed for a Cure." *Natural History*, vol. 107, 1998, pp. 22–24.

————. "Status of the Tiger in North Myanmar." *Tigerpaper*, vol. 25, 1998, pp. 15–20.

————. "Turning over a New Leaf: Muntjac Discovered in Myanmar." *Wildlife Conservation*, December 1998.

————. "The Status of the Tiger in Indochina: Separating Fact from Fiction." In J. Seidensticker, S. Christie, and P. Jackson (eds.), *Riding the Tiger: Meeting the Needs of Humans and Wildlife in Asia*. Cambridge University Press, Cambridge, 1999.

————. "Ground Truthing Conservation: Why Biological Exploration Isn't History." *Conservation in Practice*, vol. 3, 2002, pp. 20–25.

————. "A Question of Balance." *National Geographic*, vol. 205, 2004, pp. 98–117.

————. "Guns, Gold, and Greed." *Wildlife Conservation*, October 2005.

Rabinowitz, A., G. Schaller, and U Uga. "A Survey to Assess the Status of Sumatran Rhinoceros and Other Large Mammal Species in Tamanthi Wildlife Sanctuary, Myanmar." *Oryx*, vol. 29, 1995, pp. 123–128.

Rabinowitz, A., T. Myint, S. T. Khaing, and S. Rabinowitz. "Description of the Leaf Deer *(Muntiacus putaoensis)*, a New Species of Muntjac from Northern Myanmar." *Journal of Zoology*, London, vol. 249, 1999, pp. 427–435.

Rao, M., A. Rabinowitz, and S. T. Khaing. "A Status Review of the Protected Area System in Myanmar with Recommendations for Conservation Planning." *Conservation Biology*, vol. 16, 2001, pp. 360–368.

Redford, K. H. The Empty Forest. *Bioscience*, vol. 42, 1992, pp. 412–422.

Smith, J. L. D., and C. McDougal. "The Contribution of Variance in Lifetime Reproduction to Effective Population Size in Tigers." *Conservation Biology*, vol. 5, 1990, pp. 484–490.

Weatherbe, D. "Burma's Decreasing Wildlife." *Journal of the Bombay Natural History Society*, vol. 42, 1939, pp. 149–160.

Wikramanayake, E. D., E. Dinerstein, J. G. Robinson, U. Karanth, A. Rabinowitz, D. Olson, T. Mathew, P. Hedao, M. Conner, G. Hemley, and D. Bolze. "An Ecology-Based Method for Defining Priorities for Large Mammal Conservation: The Tiger as a Case Study." *Conservation Biology*, vol. 12, 1998, pp. 865–878.

Index

Note: WCS stands for Wildlife Conservation Society

Abbey, Edward, 154
Adirondack Park, 68–69
Ah Phyu, 111, 113–15, 117, 119,
    136, 182, 185, 206, 207
Air Bagan, 202
Air Myanmar, 11, 19, 129, 202
Alaungdaw Kathapa National Park,
    58–59, 95
Alexander, Jane, 82, 86
Amato, Dr. George, 44
Amber, 4, 22, 169
American Museum of Natural
    History, 44
Animal Drugs (Read), 118–19
Animal husbandry, training courses
    in, 167
Animal parts, trade in, 4, 28, 30,
    103, 113, 117, 118–20, 132
  tiger bones, 118–20
Animism, 21, 50
Ants, 169
Arachnids, 169
Art of Travel, The (de Botton), 86
Assam, Indian state of, 3, 4

Aung Leuk, 111, 112, 131, 132,
    171, 182
Aung Phone
  as minister of forestry, 69–72, 85,
    95, 127, 139, 142
  replacement as minister of
    forestry, 145
Aung San, General, 200
Aung San Suu Kyi, 144, 200
Aye Maung, Senior-General, 152
Ayeyarwady River, 54
  pollution of, 132–33

Bagan, kingdom of Burma,
    12–13
Bamah people, 161
Bamboo, 22, 46, 103
Barking deer, 27, 45, 108, 182
Ba Sein, 99
Bear, 25, 45, 113
  trade in animal parts, 103
Bees, 169
Belize, 88, 141
Berlitz, Charles, 41

Beyond the Last Village: A Journey of Discovery in Asia's Forbidden Wilderness (Rabinowitz), 14, 74, 92, 112, 129, 143
Big Game Shooting in Upper Burma (Evans), 13, 33–34
Black-necked stork, 169
Body language, 40
Britain, Southeast Asia and, 4, 12, 13, 42, 43–44, 44
Bronx Zoo
　Great Cat House at, 1–2
　Rabinowitz's office at, 75, 855
　see also Wildlife Conservation Society (WCS)
Buddhism, six levels of the cosmos in, 102
Bumphabum Wildlife Sanctuary, 149
Burma
　borders of, 4
　history of, 12–13
　independence from Britain, 43–44
　political turmoil in, 56–57
　during World War II, 4–8, 13
　see also Myanmar (formerly Burma)
Burma Independence Army, 200
Burma Road, 5, 7
Burma Surgeon Returns (Seagrave), 3, 43
Burma Wildlife Protection Act of 1936, 30
Burmese language, 40, 41
Bush, George W., 144, 172–73

Cancer, *see* Rabinowitz, Alan
Champions of the Wild, 88
Cheetahs, 120
Cheng Hlaing, Myanmar, 47
Chester Zoo, 73
Chiang Kai-shek, 5, 7, 8

China
　animal parts, trade in, 4, 28, 30, 103, 113, 118–20, 132
　cowrie shells as currency in, 52
　minerals and gems, trade in, 4
　Myanmar government and, 174
　during World War II, 5
Chindwinn River, 22, 28, 54
Chin people, 4
Chit Swe, General, 57, 70
Christianity, 20–21, 50
Chronic lymphatic leukemia, *see* Rabinowitz, Alan
Churchill, Winston, 5, 8
Clinton, Bill, administration of, 70, 144
Cobras, 47
Colinvaux, Paul, 120
Conservation
　human issues and sustainable, 92
　paradigms, 67–68
　small changes leading to lasting, 137
　struggle for, 207
"Conservation in Myanmar: Under the Gun," 173
Corbett, Jim, 32
Cowrie shells, 52

Daipha, Myanmar, 53
Daumal, René, 15–16
De Botton, Alain, 86
Deforestation, 42, 101, 102, 178
De Maistre, Xavier, 86
Department of Mines, Myanmar, 148
Duckworth, Will, 204

Eastern black-crested gibbon, 48
Economist, The, 152
Einda Sara, 92–93
Elephant Bill (Williams), 56

Elephant Preservation Act of 1879, 30

Elephants, Asian, 4, 24, 25–26, 32, 45
  declining numbers of, 29–30, 31
  described, 26
  efforts to protect Myanmar's, 30–31
  handlers (mahouts), 25
  hunting of, 28, 29–30, 113
  interaction between tigers and, 32
  for transportation, 23, 25

Evans, Major C. P., 13, 33–34

Extinct species, 120

Fisheries Department, Myanmar, 205

Fishing, dynamite, 130, 205

Forest Department, Myanmar, 11, 18, 25, 57, 58, 72, 127–28, 153, 204, 205
  director-general, 55, 62, 120, 121, 127, 128, 145, 170, 171, 201
  enforcement powers, 31
  Hponkan Razi Wildlife Sanctuary established by, 145–46
  Hukawng Valley Tiger Reserve and, 163, 205
  Hukawng Valley Tiger Reserve workshop and, 148
  land settlement issues, 147, 168, 178–79
  Northern Forest Complex and, 149
  petitioning, for protection of the Hukawng Valley, 52, 54
  socioeconomic team, 105, 130, 168
  wildlife research training courses for, 12

Fossils, new invertebrate species found in amber, 169

Friedman, Dr., 76–77, 78–79, 83

Gamebook for Burma and Adjoining Territories, A (Peacock), 13

Gaur, 27, 28, 108, 113, 179

Geographia Syntaxis (Ptolemy), 12

Global Tiger Forum, India, 57

Gold, panning for, 27, 96, 206

Gold mining, 4, 22, 96–97, 99–101, 102, 114, 117, 141, 206
  control over permits for concessions, 162, 163
  end of surge in, 169, 172
  environmental effects of, 100–101, 132–33, 162
  Hukawng Valley Tiger Reserve and, 147, 162, 163
  hunting to supply food near the mines, 108–109, 132, 171, 174

Goral, 14

Greece, ancient, 52

"Greening of a Dictatorship, The," 153

Green peafowl, 25, 169

Headhunting, 43

Hedges, Simon, 204

Himalayan "Hump," 7–8, 24, 180

Himalayas, 13, 14, 55, 91

Hkakabo Razi National Park, 145, 149

Hlawga Park, 202

Hmong people, 47

Hoolock's gibbons, 25, 48

Hornbills, 25, 133

Hponkan Razi, Myanmar, 85

Hponkan Razi Wildlife Sanctuary, 145–46, 149

Htalu people, 14

Hukawng Valley, 3–9
  history of, 3–8, 27
  human population of, 65, 67, 72, 169, 171–72

Hukawng Valley (*continued*),
 land concessions to wealthy
  Myanmar businessmen,
  191–94, 199, 201–202,
  203–204
 location of, 3
 mineral resources of, *see specific
  resources*
 original name of, 4
 size of, 65
 species richness of, 54, 168–69
 tourism in, 167–68
 as Valley of Death, 8, 9
 weather, 23, 38, 52
 wildlife in, *see specific types of
  animals*
 during World War II, 4–8, 19, 24,
  34, 50, 180, 200
Hukawng Valley Tiger Reserve, 95,
 133
 acceleration of schedule for,
  120–23
 approval of proposal for, 146
 changes in Hukawng Valley after
  conception of plan for,
  95–104, 141–42
 concept of, and reasoning behind,
  65–69, 70–72
 as conservation model, 136, 147,
  200
 criticism by opponents of
  Myanmar government of,
  173
 delineating legal extensions to the
  Hukawng Valley Wildlife
  Sanctuary, 147, 185
 development zones, 142, 163
 early planning for, 74, 85
 environmental education facility,
  151
 future of, 199, 205–207, 208
 headquarters, 151, 169–70, 179

human communities within the,
  147, 160, 163, 168, 172, 173,
  181
 KIA and, 130–37
 land concessions to wealthy
  Myanmar businessmen and,
  191–94, 199, 201–202,
  203–204
 land settlement issues, 147, 168,
  178–79, 185
 management strategy for, 148
 National Geographic article on,
  125, 131, 146
 size of, 146, 205
 tourism, 167–68
 WCS fund raising for, 172
 wildlife police force, 150–52,
  168, 170, 179, 203, 204–205,
  206
Hukawng Valley Tiger Reserve
 workshop, 2004, 148, 153, 154,
  155–56, 159–65, 180
 consensus reached at, 163
 invitees to, 148
 open discussion at, 160–62
Hukawng Valley Wildlife Sanctuary,
 65, 66, 67, 70, 95, 102
 approval of, 61–62, 64
 boundary lines for, 54, 65–66,
  112, 133, 147
 concentrating conservation efforts
  in, 110, 206
 estimates of tiger population in,
  105–107
 habitat for large vertebrates, 106
 wildlife corridors along the Ledo
  Road, 147, 192
 writing of proposal for, 55
Hungry ghosts, 102
Hunting, 27–31, 45, 117–18, 132,
 141, 205
 controls on, 142

KIA and, *see* Kachin Independent Army (KIA), hunting and
by Lisu people, *see* Lisu people, as hunters
by Naga people, *see* Naga people, as hunters
photo-trap system indicating, 107, 108, 111, 134–35
population surge in Hukawng Valley and, 102–103, 117
posting of restrictions on, 168
traditional beliefs and practices, 49–50, 114
weapons used in, 27–28, 30, 49, 102, 107, 108, 114, 174, 182, 206
see also individual species being hunter

India, 28, 57, 174
borders of, 4, 11
independence from Britain, 43–44
Naga people of, 42, 43
tiger reserves in, 106, 146, 149, 199
during World War II, 4
Indiainfo.com, 173
"Indiana Jones Meets His Match in Burma Rabinowitz," 55
Irrawaddy magazine, 153

Jadelands Company, 193, 201, 203–204
Jaguars, 88, 120, 141
Japan, World War II, and the Hukawng Valley, 4–8, 19, 24, 37, 200
Japanese language, 41–42
Javan silvery gibbon, 48
Journey around My Room, A (de Maistre), 86

Juventud Rebelde, 173

Kachin Independent Army (KIA), 20, 22, 67, 117
discussions with representatives of, 111–13, 125–26, 130–37, 182–84
gold mining and, 97, 102, 162
history of, 20
Hukawng Valley base, 20, 111, 112, 131, 132, 133, 182–84
Hukawng Valley Tiger Reserve and, 147, 153, 155–56, 159–65
hunting and, 107, 110, 111, 112, 130, 163, 167, 174, 203
loss of influence, 164
pig distribution initiative and, 167, 173, 182–83
terms of 1994 truce with Myanmar government, 162
Kachin Independent Organization (KIO), 20, 130
Central Committee of, 131, 160, 203
Hukawng Valley Tiger Reserve workshop and, 160–64
Zaung Hkra as vice chairman of, *see* Zaung Hkra
Kachin people, 4, 23, 92, 98, 134
honoring of Rabinowitz by, 184
Hukawng Valley Tiger Reserve workshop and, 161
language of, 40
during World War II, 24
Kachin State, 14, 20–21, 153
northern commander, 125–26, 129, 130–33, 151, 156, 161, 170, 171, 201, 203, 206
police chief, 170, 203
Karanth, Dr. Ullas, 57, 204
Khin Htay, 105, 108, 110, 130

Khin Maung Zaw, 55–56, 62, 71,
    95, 97
  as Director of Wildlife, 63–66, 149
  entire Hukawng Valley as tiger
    reserve, 65–66, 68, 120, 206
  Hukawng Valley Tiger Reserve
    workshop and, 160
Khin Nyunt, General
  becomes prime minister, 145
  corruption charges against, 152,
    153–54
  coup overthrowing, 152–53, 155
  Hukawng Valley Tiger Reserve
    and, 151–52.150, 155
  "road map to democracy," 145
  as Secretary-I, 122–23, 127, 128,
    131–33, 139–43
  wildlife police force and, 151–52
Krait, 47
K Seng Naw, Captain, 130–33
Kubla Khan, 13
Kumon mountain range, 149

Lamon, Myanmar, 182
Leaf deer, 45–46
  described, 44
  hunting of, 45–46, 52
Ledo Road, 5–7, 14, 20, 21, 22–23,
    25, 34, 35, 37, 98, 147
  signage concerning the tiger
    reserve, 168
Leeches, 23, 38
Leopards, 50, 56, 57, 58, 120, 179
  Hukawng Valley, 8, 25
Lesser fish-eagle, 168–69
Leukemia, see Rabinowitz, Alan
Lions, 120
Li Shih Chen, 118
Lisu people, 23, 45, 92, 98, 113–15,
    182, 185, 206
  Hukawng Valley Tiger Reserve
    workshop and, 148, 161

  as hunters, 28, 29–30, 111,
    113–15, 117–18, 119, 133,
    136, 182
  language of, 40
Lynam, Dr. Tony, 57, 58, 74, 130,
    170, 204

Macaques, 25, 45, 179
Makaw, Myanmar, 27
Malaria, 11, 24, 110, 130
Mandalay, city of, 12
Mao Tse-tung, 8
Marco Polo, 13
Medicine and medical care in
    Myanmar, 24, 92–94, 140–41,
    143, 163, 172, 173, 181,
    183
Memorial Sloan-Kettering Cancer
    Center, 17, 82–84, 123–24
Mercury, gold mining and,
    100–101, 132
Mergui Archipelago, 12
Merrill's Maruaders, 8
Methylmercury, 101
Minister of Forestry, Myanmar, 55,
    57, 201
  Aung Phone as, see Aung Phone
  Thein Aung, see Thein Aung,
    Brigadier General
Ministry of Defense, Myanmar, 17,
    132
Ministry of Mines, Myanmar, 97
Min Thein Kha, 94, 201
Mountbatten, Lord, 8
Mount Hkakabo Razi Himalayan
    region, designation as national
    park, 55
Mount Hkakabo Razi National
    Park, 61, 91
Musk deer, 14
Myanmar Air, 11, 19, 129, 202
Myanmar (formerly Burma)

anti-government activists, 92, 173
biodiversity in, 13
Black Friday, 143–44
cabinet reshuffle of August 2003, 145
coup of October 2004, 152–53, 155
government-in-exile, 173–74
Hukawng Valley, *see* Hukawng Valley
international relations, 70, 144, 172–73, 174
Kachin State, *see* Kachin State
Military Intelligence (MI), 18–19, 122, 127, 128, 139, 140, 145, 152
movement of capital of, 173–74, 200
name change to Myanmar, 13
Myanmar Northern Forest Complex, 149
Myanmar Oil and Gas Enterprise, 103, 142
Myint Maung, 95–96, 97, 130
  as chief of Hukawng Valley Tiger Reserve, 160, 168, 169–70, 180, 181, 185, 203, 204–205, 206
  as chief of Hukawng Valley Wildlife Sanctuary, 95, 110, 111, 114
  meetings with KIO authorities, 160
  tiger survey team, 105, 106, 107, 130
  wildlife police force and, 151–52, 170, 205
Myint Thein, Lieutenant Colonel, 129, 132
Myin Yang, 100
Myitkyina, Myanmar, 18, 19–20, 94–95, 129, 130

Hukawng Valley Tiger Reserve workshop in, 159–65, 180

Naga Hills, 34, 35, 43, 44, 47, 145, 179–81, 205
Naga people, 5, 12, 23, 35, 42–52, 180–82
  depiction of, 180–81
  headhunting by, 43
  Hukawng Valley Tiger Reserve workshop and, 148, 161, 180
  human sacrifice by, 44
  as hunters, 49–50, 113–14, 182
  language of, 40
Namdapha National Park, 149
Namyun, Myanmar, 35, 42–47, 51–52, 179–80
National Coalition Government of the Union of Burma, 173–74
National Geographic, 125, 131, 146
National League for Democracy, 144, 145
National Socialist Council of Nagaland, 42
National Tiger Action Plans, 57, 58, 64, 66, 70
National Tiger Survey Team, 58, 74, 95, 105, 130
  report of, 64
  training of, 58–59, 95
Native Tongues (Berlitz), 41
Nature, 173
Nay Pyi Taw, Myanmar, 200–201
Ne Win, General, 56–57
New Light of Myanmar, The, 122, 191
New York Botanical Garden, 168
New York Times, 55
Nimer, Dr. Stephen, 82–84, 124, 174
Nobel Peace Prize, 144

Nocturnal Expedition around My Room (de Maistre), 86
Northern Forest Complex, Myanmar, 149
North Korea, 140

Ohn Myint, Major General, 203
Oil and gas exploration, 103, 142, 169
Opium, 24, 25, 57
Orchids, 38, 39
Otters, 28, 113

Palaung people, 4
Pangsaung Pass, 35, 37
  talk of reopening of, 173
Pascal, Blaise, 86
Patkai Mountain Range, 4, 11, 37
Peacock, E. H., 13
Peking Natural History Bulletin, 118
Pensées (Pascal), 86
Pen Tsao Kang Mu (The Great Herbal, 118
Pheasant, 45
Plato, 125
Pneumonia, 48
Poole, Colin, 204
Protection of Wildlife Law of 1994, 31
Ptolemy, 12
Pumas, 120
Putao, Myanmar, 13, 15, 28, 56, 113
  Buddhist monastery in, 92–93
  WCS environmental education center in, 91–92
Pyinmana, Myanmar, 174
Pythons, 179

Rabinowitz, Alana Jane (daughter), 86–87

Rabinowitz, Alan (author)
  Beyond the Last Village, 14, 74, 92, 112, 129, 143
  childhood stuttering, 1–2, 40, 88
  family life, 73–76, 81, 86–89, 157–59, 187–91, 197–98
  first two years in Myanmar, 12, 14–15
  grief counseling, 81–82
  health problems, 76–84, 85, 87, 92–94, 123–25, 140–41, 143, 159, 174, 185, 189, 201
  Hukawng Valley Tiger Reserve and, *see* Hukawng Valley Tiger Reserve
  Myanmar officials and, *see specific agencies and individuals*
  parents of, 187–91, 197–98
  on travel, 86
  WCS field staff, sense of responsibility for, 144
Rabinowitz, Alexander (son), 73, 75, 81, 87–89, 158–59, 187
Rabinowitz, Salisa (wife), 44, 61, 73–76, 78, 79, 81, 82, 86–89, 144, 157, 158, 189, 191, 197
Rattan, 22, 103
  cultivation of, 168
Rawang people, 14, 92
Read, Bernard, 118
Red pandas, 14
Rice, 23, 27, 46, 181
Roosevelt, Franklin D., 5, 7, 8
Russell's viper, 47
Russia, 174

Sambar deer, 27, 45, 179, 182, 206
  diet of tigers and, 102–103, 108, 109, 135
  hunting of, 102–103, 108–109, 135, 163, 167, 171
Sandflies, 169

Sangpawng Mountains, 11
San Lwin, Police Colonel, 203
Sariska tiger reserve, 199
Saw Htoo Tha Po, 105, 106, 107, 111, 160
Saw Lwin, 38, 39, 40, 42, 53
Saw Tun Khaing, 17, 26–27, 32, 38, 48, 51, 54, 55, 58, 63, 130, 141, 143
  changes in Hukawng Valley and, 97, 101, 102
  diary of, 39
  entire Hukawng Valley as tiger reserve and, 72, 120–21
  monkhood, departure from WCS to enter, 121–22, 148–49
  Myanmar program for WCS and, 11, 18, 61–62, 64, 65, 128, 129, 130, 133, 136, 139, 140
  painting of a tiger given to Alan Rabinowitz, 148–49
  short-term generosity and, 26, 46
  traditional medicine and, 93–94
  as translator, 41, 49, 112, 113, 137
Schaller, Dr. George, 85
Seagrave, Dr. Gordon, 3, 43
September 11, 2001, 75–76
Serow, 179
Shan people, 4, 23
  Hukawng Valley Tiger Reserve workshop and, 148, 161
  language of, 40
Sherrin, Ed, 86
Shinbweyan, Myanmar, 30, 34–36, 53, 105, 179, 182
  changes in, 99–102
  gold mining in, 99, 100, 169, 206
  travel to, 98–99
Slash-and-burn agriculture, 21, 47, 49, 133, 181
Snow leopards, 120
South Korea, 140

Spot-billed pelican, 25
State Law and Order Restoration Council (SLORC), 140
State Peace and Development Council (SPDC), 140, 145
Stilwell, General "Vinegar" Joe, 3, 5–7, 43
Stuttering, see Rabinowitz, Alan
Sumatran rhinos, 12, 18
Swidden agriculture, see Slash-and-burn agriculture

Tailings, mining, 101
Takin, 14
Tamanthi Wildlife Sanctuary, 18–19, 28, 56
Tanai River, 22, 53, 133, 183
  new bridge across, 96, 97, 117
Tanai (Tanai township), Myanmar, 20, 29–30, 53, 54, 67, 162, 204
  aid for local people of, 163
  changes in, 96–98, 141, 169
  described, 21–22
  enclosed by Hukawng Valley Tiger Reserve, 147
  land settlement issues and, 178–79, 185
Taron people, 14
Taron River, 98–99
Tawang Bum mountain range, 37
Tawang River, 98–99, 103
Thai Airways, 197
Than Myint, 18, 35–36, 41, 54, 55, 63, 64, 96, 97, 204
  coup of October 2004 and, 153, 154
  Hukawng Valley Tiger Reserve and, 74, 121–22, 125–26, 128, 129, 130, 148, 150, 156, 162, 163, 164, 191–92, 194, 200–202, 208

226   Index

Than Myint (*continued*),
  takes over from Saw Tun Khaing,
    148
  wildlife police force and, 151–52,
    170
Than Shwe, General, 145, 152,
  155
Thein Aung, Brigadier General, 39
  as minister of forestry, 145, 146,
    148, 150–51, 154–56, 170,
    192–94, 201–202
Thura Shwe Mann, General, 152
Tiger habitat, worldwide, 199–200
Tigers in the wild, 2006 report on,
  199–200
Tigers of Hukawng Valley, 4, 8, 14,
  15, 34–35, 46–47, 56, 74
  declining numbers of, 29
  estimates of number of, 105–107
  Hukawng Valley Tiger Reserve,
    see Hukawng Valley Tiger
    Reserve
  Hukawng Valley Wildlife
    Sanctuary, *see* Hukawng Valley
    Wildlife Sanctuary
  human encounters and sightings,
    33–34, 169, 182, 206, 207
  hunting of, 28, 45, 46–47, 49–50,
    52, 64, 109, 113, 114, 117,
    118, 132, 167, 173
  Naga were-tigers, 35, 49–50
  photo-trap system to investigate,
    74, 105–108, 109, 110, 111,
    134–35, 160, 174
  prey depletion, 102–103, 108,
    109–10, 112
  as proxy of healthy environment,
    54–55
  reproduction by, 109
  tracks and tracking, 25, 31–33,
    50
  traditional beliefs about, 49–50

Tigers of Myanmar
  declining numbers of, 56, 57–58,
    64
  in Hukawng Valley, *see* Tigers of
    Hukawng Valley
  National Tiger Survey Team, *see*
    National Tiger Survey Team
  in 1800s, 56
Tin Win Tun, Chief, 204–205
Tizzard, Rob, 204
Tourism, 167–68
Translators, 41
  nuances of language and, 41–42
Tuberculosis, 24, 48
Tu Ja, Dr., 203
Tun Paw OO, 202
Turtles, 28

Uga, U, 55, 63
United Nations Development
  Programme, 122, 163
  Hukawng Valley Tiger Reserve
    workshop and, 148
U.S. Treasury Department, Office
  of Foreign Assets Control, 144

Voice Crying in the Wilderness, A
  (Abbey), 154
Voice of America, 153

Wheeler, Lieutenant General
  Raymond, 37
White-bellied heron, 25, 169
White-winged wood duck, 25,
  168
Why Big Fierce Animals Are Rare
  (Colinvaux), 120
Wildlife Conservation Society
  (WCS), 18, 95, 105, 140, 160,
  202, 204
  coup in Myanmar in October
    2004 and, 153

Hukawng Valley Tiger Reserve
    and, *see* Hukawng Valley Tiger
    Reserve
Putao environmental education
    center, 91–92
sanctions on Myanmar and, 144
Thailand Program, 57
see also Bronx Zoo
Wildlife police force, Hukawng
    Valley Tiger Reserve, 150–52,
    168, 170, 179, 203, 204–205,
    206
Wild pig and wild boar, 25, 27, 45,
    49, 179, 182, 206
    diet of tigers and, 102–103, 108,
        109, 135
    distribution of fast-breeding
        domestic piglets, 167, 173,
        182–83
    hunting of, 108–109, 135, 163,
        167, 171
Williams, Lieutenant Colonel J. H.,
    56
Wingate, General Orde Charles, 8
Winter, Steve, 125, 131, 146

Woolly-necked stork, 25
Wordsworth, William, 189
Workshop, Hukawng Valley Tiger
    Reserve, *see* Hukawng Valley
    Tiger Reserve workshop
World War II, 13, 24, 37
    Hukawng Valley during, 4–8, 19,
        34, 50, 180, 200

Yangon, Myanmar, 13, 139, 200
    bomb attack of 1983 by North
        Korean agents, 140
    moving of capital to Pyinmana
        from, 173–74, 200
    Shwedagon Pagoda, 178
    WCS offices in, 127
Yangon Zoo, 45
Yaung Ngwe, Myanmar, 180–82
Yee, David, 87
Yup Zaw Hkawng, 201
Yuzana Corporation, 193, 202

Zaung Hkra, 160, 161, 164–65,
    170, 171, 203
Zoraptera, 169

About the Author

Alan Rabinowitz is executive director of the Science and Exploration Program for the Wildlife Conservation Society. Educated at the University of Tennessee, with degrees in zoology and wildlife ecology, Dr. Rabinowitz has traveled the world on behalf of wildlife conservation and has studied jaguars, clouded leopards, Asiatic leopards, tigers, Sumatran rhinos, bears, leopard cats, raccoons, and civets.

His work in Belize resulted in the world's first jaguar sanctuary; his work in Taiwan resulted in the establishment of that country's largest protected area, its last piece of intact lowland forest; his work in Thailand generated the first field research on Indochinese tigers, Asiatic leopards, and leopard cats, in what was to become the region's first World Heritage Site; and his work in Myanmar has led to the creation of five new protected areas there: the country's first marine national park, the country's first and largest Himalayan national park, the country's largest wildlife sanctuary, and the world's largest tiger reserve.

Dr. Rabinowitz has authored nearly eighty scientific and popular articles and six other books, including *Jaguar: One Man's Struggle to Establish the World's First Jaguar Preserve* (1986/2000), *Chasing the Dragon's Tail: The Struggle to Save Thailand's Wild Cats* (1991/2002), and *Beyond the Last Village: A Journey of Discovery in Asia's Forbidden Wilderness* (2001). He has been profiled in the *New York Times, Scientific American, Audubon, Men's Journal, Outside, Explorer,* the *Jerusalem Report, Christian Science Monitor,* and *National Geographic Adventure Magazine,* and is the subject of the acclaimed PBS/*National Geographic* television special *In Search of the Jaguar.*